Guns Above, Steam Below in Canada's Navy of WWII

A.G.W. LAMONT

HMCS *Qu'Appelle*, *H 69*, *in company with* **HMCS** *Skeena* *to the south of Iceland,*
the morning of **Skeena***'s last day at sea.*
24 October 1944.
Painting by David Davies ("Jasper"), 1993.

Guns Above, Steam Below

in Canada's Navy of W.W.II

A.G.W. Lamont

with parts from
R. Brooks,
H. Dadson,
A. Gillespie,
G. Stone,
R. Telford

Foreword by
LtCmdr A. Easton, DSC, RCN(R) (Ret'd)

Published by

MELROSE BOOKS

An Imprint of Melrose Press Limited
St Thomas Place, Ely
Cambridgeshire
CB7 4GG, UK
www.melrosebooks.com

First published by A.G.W. Lamont 2003
This Edition published by Melrose Books 2006

Copyright © A. G. W. Lamont 2002

The Author asserts his moral right to
be identified as the author of this work

Cover designed by Geoff Hobbs Design

ISBN 1 905226 60 8

Printed and bound in Great Britain by:

CONTENTS

v

Foreword

Alan Easton,

Lieutenant Commander, DSC, RCN(R) (Ret'd)
Author of
"50 North, Canada's Atlantic Battleground"

VOLUMES HAVE BEEN WRITTEN ABOUT THE STRUGGLE of the Royal Canadian Navy in the war which most of us can still remember, the long-dragged out Battle of the Atlantic, our skirmishes in the West Indies, the Mediterranean and finally the English Channel. The engagements depicted were usually detection of the unseen enemy lurking under the dark waters, the sharp upper deck action with guns and underwater explosions. We have read most of these dramatic occasions well told and true; but curiously almost nothing has been written about those men pinned below decks who had to provide the vital driving power of the ship. They heard the bomb and felt the shock which shook the hull, but knew nothing.

Here at last is one, "Guns Above, Steam Below; in the Canadian Navy of WWII", which describes what went on in the hot, noise-ridden caverns in the bowels of the ship, the engine room and the boiler room at the bottom of a shaft, and the men who knew nothing of what was taking place above them or beneath the keel yet knew the danger by the very manoeuvres they were ordered to carry out.

Archie Lamont, engineer lieutenant in a destroyer during the Normandy invasion, has written a most interesting and sensitive account of the part played by **HMCS** *Qu'Appelle*, the leader of a force of four Canadian destroyers. Graduating the year before in engineering from the University of Toronto, he was eagerly taken at once by the Navy, and drawn into the management of boiler water so that ships might keep the sea longer. If this subject sounds boring to anyone but an engineer, it is not; the author has written about it without dwelling extensively on the complexities of a ship's engine, or even his steam boilers. Rather, he relates a human story of people in a wartime naval environment, and the variety of their character and disposition.

Qu'Appelle was brought in from the Atlantic to establish one more small force of four Canadian destroyers to join the greatest sea-borne invasion of all time and was at the western entrance to the Channel on June 6, when the famous D-Day dawned. Lamont describes how those at the engine room controls below were aware of the chase going on above by the frequent changes in speed and the thud of exploding depth charges astern, and of torpedoes and glider bombs near by. He takes us through two swift, 30 knot, close-range night engagements with well-armed German surface vessels.

With this volume, another spoke has turned in the wheel of naval history.

Alan Easton was Commanding Officer of **HMCS Saskatchewan**, one of the ships of EG12 led by **HMCS Qu'Appelle** Earlier he had commanded three other smaller vessels, including the renowned corvette **HMCS Sackville** now lying at Halifax. He exemplified perfectly the qualities of leadership celebrated in this book. He died aged 100 in September of the year 2001.

DEDICATION

These hearts were woven of human joys and cares,
Washed marvellously with sorrow, swift to mirth,
The years had given them kindness. Dawn was theirs;
And sunset, and the colours of the earth.

Rupert Brooke

Dawn, too, is ours, and sunset, and the colours of the earth, but eventually we must join those who have fallen in the past, some in battle, some in the ways of a peaceful life. Many of those who have gone ahead sacrificed themselves for us, for those who are living now. In Canada, benefiting from our great good fortune in having a thousand year tradition of increasing rejection of oppressive authority at home and tyranny abroad, we have reached a condition in which man need not fear those in charge.

This book is dedicated to all who have brought us to, and maintained us in, this condition, especially those of the Royal Canadian Navy. Additionally, it is dedicated to a specific one of those people, to the man who, at the time I knew him, was LtCommander (E) I.J.L. Palmer, Royal Canadian Naval Reserve.

It is written by one who experienced none of the horrors of the poet's 1914–1918 war, nor touched on any of the equally terrible experiences of some in the 1939–1945 war. By contrast, my experiences verged on the idyllic. However, they were those of one man, by lot, and that one man an engineer to boot. Here

they are, some to laugh at, and some to cry about—
and with some to do neither. Keep in mind:

> *"Whatever happens is as common and well-known as a rose*
> *in spring or an apple in autumn—everywhere, up and down,*
> *ages and histories, towns and families, are full of the same*
> *stories."*
>
> **(Attributed to Antonius Pius; more I know not.)**

1. HITLER'S WAR COMES

In dreary, doubtful, waiting hours,
before the brazen frenzy starts,
"Into Battle" Julian Grenfell

GERMANY IN 1933, SUFFERING FROM MASSIVE
UNEMPLOYMENT (as was all the world, in fact) and
thinking itself ill-done by as an outcome of WWI,
elected the Nazi party to power. A few months later
Adolph Hitler, head of the Nazi party, was appointed
Chancellor of the Third Reich, and Germany began
to lead the world down the trail to disaster. Hitler was
devoted to the idea of world domination by Germany,
and intended war to bring it about. He found eager
helpers to do the things necessary for war and, despite
treaties, agreements, objections, Germany began to
rearm in earnest, building particularly its armies and
its air force.

But the navy, the Reichsmarine (State Navy), was
not overlooked; renamed the Kriegsmarine (Combat
Navy) it began to organize into two arms, one made up
of heavy surface ships and the other of a submarine (U-
boat) force. The surface ships, championed by Admiral
Eric Raeder, were of a "classical" nature, battleships,
cruisers, destroyers, intended to engage similar forces
from France, Poland, and Heaven forbid, Britain.
Raeder considered his surface ships as able commerce

raiders, as well as being competent to engage similar enemy vessels. The submarine arm, attracting much smaller sums of money, was directed by a man who had been converted to the belief that the only hope in a war with Britain, which he considered inevitable, was the submarine, sailed against commerce with the clear objective of strangling Britain's commercial lifeline across the Atlantic. So began the world-shaking career of Karl Dönitz, who eventually became Chancellor of Germany on Hitler's death. He was fanatical in his belief in the U-boat, and was victorious in his promotion of the U-boat arm of the Kriegsmarine when the German surface fleet had been, effectively, destroyed. Besides, Dönitz really had Hitler on his side, a Hitler who loved armies and air power, but who was contemptuous of conventional seagoing forces, whether called the Kriegsmarine or not.

The first U-boat, U1, was commissioned in June of 1935. Hitler planned for no extensive war until the mid-1940s, by which time expansion of the surface and submarine fleets would be just about complete. In the event, his war started much earlier, in September of 1939, at which time the number of U-boats that Germany was able to have on patrol at sea was only about twenty. The number to be deployed by war's end amounted to over 1,200.

Dönitz's emphasis in his U-boat strategy was the destruction of merchant vessels, and his tactics centred around the marshalling of a group of U-boats by radioed instructions and guidance from his command centre ashore. The British reaction to the U-boat threat was the organization of merchant vessels into convoys, groups of around 100 ships sailing together under escort by a few warships. The warships had the task of forcing the U-boats to submerge, and thereby to frustrate their attack and to cause them to lose contact with the convoy. Should a U-boat be destroyed in the process, that was all to the good, but the primary aim was to get the ships of the convoy safely through to ports in Britain. By March 1941, over 600 merchant vessels had been lost to U-boats while fewer than 15 of the predators had been destroyed by British forces, leading Churchill to proclaim the "Battle of the Atlantic", and to write years later that the shipping situation was his biggest worry during the war.

Canada entered the war with a minuscule navy, with under 5,000 people and about a dozen warships. The beginning of war brought with it a frenzied program of construction in both Canada and Britain of small warships, the now-famous corvettes, conceived at first as suitable for the waters around Britain, where the U-boats were initially active. About a thousand tons of displacement, two hundred feet long, and carrying lots of depth charges, corvettes were one of the most successful vessels ever built in terms of their ability to do what they were intended for, and more. Their working area was extended further and further out to sea as the U-boats penetrated further and further west, eventually covering the whole North Atlantic, where they were indeed miserable ships for the crews, especially in the winter, for they were cramped, small, rolled horribly, iced up easily (becoming unstable), and were generally hell. But, in the main, reliable.

By the end of the war there were over 100,000

people and hundreds of warships, most of them corvettes, in the RCN. Canadian shipyards built hundreds of them including small numbers of minesweepers and a few destroyers. Naval Service headquarters in Ottawa were overwhelmed with the chaotic problems this flood of ships presented. Ships need men to run them, instruments to guide them, weapons to fight them. Gyro compasses were essential, but for long unavailable. It is said that some Canadian ships went to sea with dummy guns in place; ships' crews just learning to work a ship were decimated in favour of sending them to man other new ones, so preventing the development of teamwork on board any ship. Along with help from the USA, Canada had been assigned the task of containing the U-boats in the western Atlantic. The consequence of the extreme need for convoy escorts, and the extreme shortage of experienced men, suitable instruments, and weapons was utter failure on the part of Canada, leading to a withdrawal of Canadian forces from convoy activities for a short time. Returning to the task after a reasonable period of proper training, they did magnificently. Magnificently, despite instrumental handicaps that were persistent.

By the end of 1943, it was patently obvious to the senior officers of the Wehrmacht (the German army) that the war was lost. On 20 July of 1944 some of them even tried to stop it by killing Hitler; they failed and met terrible retribution. But Hitler continued his now hopeless war, with a determination that Germany itself and its people should pay dearly for their failure to support him properly. Grand Admiral Dönitz from the earliest days of his service in the submarine arm of the Reichsmarine had seen the role of the U-boat as the strangulation of British commerce at sea. In March of 1941 he had seemed well on his way to doing just that, leading to Churchill's deepest fears. But the Battle of the Atlantic proclaimed by Churchill, bringing greatly increased aerial measures and much better naval forces, changed the picture totally. Many ships were still being lost, but by the end of 1943 it was clear to all that Dönitz's objective could not be fulfilled; British commerce could not possibly be strangled by the U-boats. Any ship lost by the Allies after the end of 1943 was a grievous individual loss, but such losses had no effect on the outcome of the war one way or another. Nevertheless Dönitz continued to send his crews to sea, in a persistence toward a defeated goal that the author considers tantamount to murderous, both of the U-boat crews themselves and of their continuing victims. Dönitz faced prosecution at Nuremberg for his part in an aggressive war, and was convicted on two of three charges. He should have been indicted also for his post-1943 objectives, which were simply to sink whatever could be sunk.

Some of his U-boat captains were engaged also in what must be seen as murder. Consider the case of U-190 under Hans Edwin Reith, 24 years of age, in his first command. Twenty-two days before the formal end of the war Reith had not sunk a single vessel, couldn't bear the thought, and sank **HMCS** *Esquimalt* to avoid this blot on his own escutcheon. Reith killed 39 men for his own "glory" only; the sinking had no purpose as far as the war was concerned.

This account describes two and a half years as an engineer in the Royal Canadian Navy during WWII, experiencing the realities of men, guns, and steam at war, and of the eternal aspects of sea and sky. Until recently, GUNS were the only or principal offensive weapon carried by warships over a period of a few hundred years. In World War II, the gun still characterized the offensive power of the ships of the Allied navies, and certainly those of Canada's navy, though most of them actually fired far more depth charges than they did artillery rounds. Those days are now long gone, and guns are truly of little importance, their type of offensive abilities having been replaced almost entirely by rockets. STEAM as the medium of power in ships has gone through a similar change, though in a much shorter time. First used to drive ships in the early 1800s it was still preeminent in WWII when most of the ships of Canada's wartime Navy did indeed employ steam engines. Today, like the gun, steam has also become an anachronism at sea, replaced by internal combustion engines of various kinds (except in nuclear submarines).

Steam at sea brought with it the need for engineers in the ships. At the time of the Great Armada in 1588 navies carried two kinds of men on board their ships, the mariners who worked the ship, and the gunners who worked the guns and fought it. Over two hundred years later at Trafalgar in 1805, the manning of warships was still much the same, though the mariners and gunners were now one group. But profound change was about to take place—mechanical power would replace the wind in driving vessels, and engineers became necessary to look after the machinery. They first went to sea in the Royal Navy in **HMS *Lightning*** which appeared in the Navy List in 1828, only a quarter of a century after Trafalgar, the first steam-driven vessel in that service. Those who looked after boilers and engines were initially considered civilians, and were bitterly resented by the military officers. From that beginning, in which engineers ranked "with, but after carpenters", they rose steadily in status in the Royal Navy, until accorded military rank in 1925 when their organization was finally formalized into that which existed during WWII. Had Samuel Pepys, with his organizing genius, still lived the new problems brought by the engineers would no doubt have been solved much earlier.

The Royal Canadian Navy, established by Act of Parliament in 1910, was modelled meticulously on the Royal Navy in almost all its detail. For five hundred years, ending about the time that US maritime supremacy was demonstrated in the great naval battles of the Pacific war in the 1940s, the Royal Navy kept the world in order. Its ships and men, from the time of the Spanish Armada, and reorganized into its final form by the great Pepys, ranged far and wide and were known to all centres of power. The culmination and ultimate demonstration of its importance came at Trafalgar. There, one of its admirals, revered for ever by his countrymen, began the release of the world from its first modern tyranny. A hundred and a quarter years passed before another equally terrible threat had to be dealt with by Britain and its allies, and the Battle of the Atlantic was mounted. That battle was even more crucial and much more protracted than Trafalgar, and was itself a great endeavour. In that great endeavour the Royal Canadian Navy was of crucial importance, backing up and supplementing the Royal Navy itself at every possible turn. At the time this story opens, expansion of the RCN was very well advanced, and it had become a force to be reckoned with at sea.

The crews of the U-boats included many very brave men, but men who were unaware, or uncaring of the depth of that evil of which they were agents. Allied forces were responsible for the destruction of hundreds of U-boats and of their crews, and of other vessels, and we have to thank God for it. Had the U-boats prevailed, the world would have become a far different place. During their attempt at world domination, the forces of darkness and evil managed to kill millions of innocents. Had the Nazi agents prevailed, the whole of the Jewish, Gypsy, disadvantaged and various other groups would soon have been killed. Those who served in the Royal Canadian Navy can be proud of their part in the destruction of the Nazi evil.

Late in April of 1943, finished with the study of Chemical Engineering at the University of Toronto, the author was commissioned into the Royal Canadian Naval Service as a Probationary Acting Temporary Sub Lieutenant (E). The E stood for Engineering, one of those modern branches into which the Navy was divided; Probationary meant Learn Fast and Be Careful or out you go, Acting meant Tolerated by the Establishment, and Temporary meant Wartime

Helper.

In contributing to the utter defeat of Dönitz and the German U-boats, Canada, fortunately, had many great leaders at sea, serving in ranks high and low. This book tells about some of them.

THE QUALITY OF LEADERSHIP is mentioned in several places in this book. On this page is the first part of an excerpt of a poem by our own Joseph Schull, the very Joseph who was commissioned in the late 1940s to write the official history of the Navy at war ("The Far Distant Ships"). The excerpt is from his "The Legend of Ghost Lagoon". The excerpt is included here because it is an interesting description of one of the qualities of leadership in action at sea, albeit of the leader of a group of buccaneers, Solomon Sleavy. He and his crew sailed the **Lady Kate**:

> *... The warm sun poured,*
> *A winsome breeze in the rigging snored,*
> *The bright foam leaped on the sapphire sea,*
> *They drove on their course right merrily*
> *And doom and death from their minds far-rolled*
> *Lean heavily down on their fortunate keel.*
> *A cheerful oath or a song would steal*
> *To their lips as now with the nearing goal*
> *The pictured joys of their wealth unroll. ...*

2. HMCS COBALT AND BOILER WATERS

Does he need you at his side?
You can start this very evening if you choose,
And take the Western Ocean in the stride
Of seventy thousand horses and some screws!
"The Secret of the Machines" R. Kipling

The story is continued at the end of Chapter 2

HIS MAJESTY'S CANADIAN SHIP COBALT WAS A CORVETTE, commissioned in 1940, one of 123 in the RCN (121 of them built in Canada), almost a thousand tons of displacement, two hundred feet long, with only one 4 inch gun, one two pounder gun, and two half inch guns—but many depth charges. In an attack on a U-boat, four depth charges were discharged from throwers to the beam of the vessel by a kind of gun (mortar), another six being dropped over the stern while the vessel hurried on to be out of the influence of the resulting explosions.

Cobalt, as were a number of other corvettes, was

engaged in ploughing the waters of the Triangle Run—Halifax, New York, St John's, escorting convoys. Month after month and year after year she went from one to the other of her three ports. She had a relatively uneventful time, surviving storm, and fog, and ice, leaving behind no events of enough significance to merit an entry in any index of the many books referred to later in this particular one. Unpunctuated repetition, almost boredom, was her lot. But her crews are to be seen as some of the heroes of the Royal Canadian Navy, fulfilling their role of seeing to it that the merchant ships got through to Britain, discouraging and frustrating U–boat attacks.

Her Captain

Commanded by Lt Ronald Judges, RCNVR, *Cobalt* to the time I joined in mid-1943 had had an uneventful war. But not long after I left the ship, Judges was mentioned in dispatches, one of his officers, Mate Bett, RCNR, was awarded the George Medal, and two ratings, ERA Werely and Signalman Fitzgerald, the British Empire Medal, for their actions in putting out a fire in a US tanker at sea. Judges was a former yachtsman from the National Yacht Club in Toronto. As a yachtsman he, and many like him in the RCNVR, had sailed boats of the order of perhaps 30 ft or 40 ft in length, and a few tons in weight. With what trepidation, in their

Toronto Evening Telegram, 1943 Nov. 20

early days on the bridge of a warship, must those of them who assumed command have approached the dock with a corvette, over 200 ft in length and a thousand tons of moving threat to any dock made! Judges, who had joined the ship only a few weeks earlier, was good at it—as those of us in the engine room could recognize from the orders coming from the bridge. Fortunately, he didn't object to the presence of supernumerary officers on board. Later that year, out of Prince Rupert, two different Captains were encountered, one of them totally unfriendly, and the other the soul of fun and good spirits; not all captains were alike. Some, unlike Judges, did indeed take objection to supernumeraries like me, if only because they added pressure to an already cramped and tense situation.

Bridge Watches with Mate Bett

Toronto Evening Telegram, 1943 Nov. 20

Cobalt was short of officers, and it was soon realized that duties in the Boiler Water business in the engine room were not onerous, and could be dealt with in a few hours during the day. So the Boiler Water man was pre-empted (voluntarily) for watch-keeping duties on the bridge, on the upper deck, the domain of the Guns, far removed from the Steam Below—though he was but an engineer officer, and "acting" to boot, and only seven weeks in the Naval Service at that! I stood watch with Mate Bett, a very patient human being, who taught me and showed me anything I wanted or needed. He was later to become Commanding Officer of **Cobalt** when Judges moved on to another command.

Mate Bett was in the Royal Canadian Naval Reserve, a small group of professional seamen— fishermen, merchantmen, bootleggers even, men who knew the sea intimately from years of experience, and had committed themselves in times of peace to serve the nation in the Navy should war come about. Bett was a highly able naval officer, as well as being a professional seaman. Of his kind, those who held ocean-going certificates from the merchant service entered the Naval Reserve with the ranks of Sub Lt, Mate, Chief Skipper, or Lieutenant. Like its progenitor, the Royal Navy, the Royal Canadian Navy was elitist in outlook, for reservists who were yachtsmen moved higher in rank and faster, in general, than their professional colleagues who had been 'only' fishermen or merchantmen.

Many of the watches with Mate Bett were at night, and the attractions of the sea with its beauty and mystery began to be understood. On some of those watches, at night, the sky was cloudless, clear, and totally dark but for the stars. Bett gave his colleagues on the bridge a first experience in the naming of the stars and constellations, and the sky always had a more glorious appearance for such instructions. Then there were the night watches in waters infested with icebergs, watching and waiting tensely for the sight of one, ready at an instant to holler down the wheelhouse voice pipe to the engine room "Full

Speed Astern". We saw them, but fortunately never struck one.

The most moving of experiences at sea starts before the least sign of dawn in the blackness and the endlessness of the night. Tired, one thinks that night has now been ordained as everlasting and forever, and the blackness invades the soul. Time loses meaning, and the dim redness from the binnacle does nothing but emphasize the surrounding nothingness. In the depths of despair the realization comes strangely and suddenly that there is a faint greyness to the surrounding murk, a greyness that was not there, and that disjoints one's immediate perceptions. The greyness grows, and ghostly figures appear out of the darkness on the bridge, the ghostly figures of shipmates. It grows, and their images strengthen. Then, it may be that the fog lifts, and the eastern sky lightens and colours. One morning, after a foggy night, this very thing happened, and "The sun he rose upon the right, Out of the sea came he ...." It was a dark red through the remnant haze, sitting on dark red gossamer-like clouds, and splashing a glorious red spot on the oily ocean. There is nothing to match sunrise at sea.

Some things come close, though. Whales blowing and playing. White foam and waves dashing against brown unyielding rock rimming an emerald sea. High headlands silhouetted starkly against a sunset sky, each successive rank of land greyer than the one ahead. The moon, large and round and mystic, rising slowly and wonderfully from behind a bank of clouds. At sea the wonders are endless, and finely focused from being concentrated into the basic simplicity of sea and sky.

Then we came upon New York—the ***Ambrose*** lightship far out, the various buoys and lights winking redly or greenly as we made our way in the dark, Mate Bett giving instructions on what to look for. It was a profound experience, a magic one for the first time at sea. And then New York itself! On shore leave, we crossed in the Staten Island Ferry, past the Statue of Liberty, onto the subway, noisy and dirty and exciting, out to Times Square. And in Times Square, everything began to rock and roll and the Boiler Water man came closer to being seasick than ever again, whether ashore or at sea.

Our return from New York had its own excitement and new experience. The convoy had us and a destroyer as escort, and one of the crew aboard the destroyer became very seriously ill. We were instructed to take him off and return as quickly as possible to port with him. Transfers of people at sea are not everyday occurrences and are full of interest. Fortunately the weather was not terrible, though foggy, as the two ships steamed side by side at a distance of a few dozen feet, rolling in the swell, white water being knifed aside by the destroyer's sharp bow. In the dense fog and drizzling rain, with a flurry of signals rattling back and forth, the sick man got transferred by breeches buoy, and off we went. Off we went at high speed, in fact, fog or no fog.

There were other experiences of a curious nature in ***Cobalt***. MacMillan, one of the RCNVR deck officers, and I one day got into the ammunition magazine, and removed the fuses from shells for two of the Guns Above, a 25 mm and an Oerlikon, and melted out the explosive charges. To remember the day is to tremble.

What Made *Cobalt* Move

Most tales of the Navy tell about the people and show pictures of the ships as they appear to the outsider, lying or moving in the water. Few indeed tell or show what made them move. It was the engine room department which made them move, operating with engines and boilers and fuel oil. "Fuel oil" immediately suggests fire and heat. The engines in ships and trains and

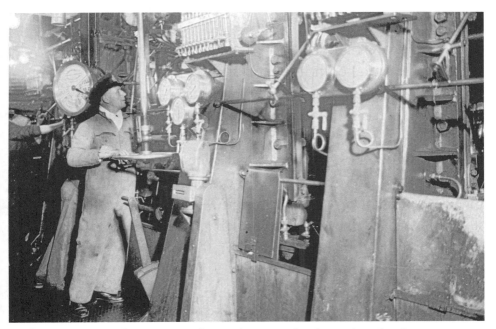

In the engine room, showing part of an engine somewhat larger than that in a corvette. Hand is on the throttle. Telegraph from the bridge behind his head. Reversing lever in front of left leg. Lubricatng sight indicators at top mid-left. Two columns on mid-right hold up cylinders. At bottom between columns are oil-splash boards. National Maritime Museum (NMM) A17874

planes and autos are, plainly, heat engines. Supplied
with heat in the proper way, they change part of it
(about a third only) into mechanical motion to drive
the ship, and must throw out the other part (about
two thirds). The proportions seem wasteful, but the
laws of the universe make them unavoidable except
to a minor extent.

Steam, steam, glo————r-i-ous steam! The first
medium ever used for converting heat into mechanical
motion was steam—starting with the toy invented
by Hero of Alexandria. His toy came to nothing of
importance, but two thousand years later, inventive
men in Europe made steam into a source of wealth
and power. By the early 1800s its use had spread from
pumping water in mines to driving vessels at sea, and
ideas for its use at sea continued to develop over a
period of more than a hundred years. Initially paddle
wheels were the common last stage of the driving
process. Their use didn't last, and screw propellers
took their place (very slowly and cautiously, it might
be said, in the Royal Navy!), but whether paddles
or screw propellers, the rotational speed needed was
relatively low. There are two choices for developing a
given amount of power in an engine—big, heavy, and
slow, or small, light, and fast, and the development of
the kind of engine used in **Cobalt** followed the big,
heavy, and slow route.

Corvettes were driven by the expansion of steam
in triple-expansion reciprocating engines, beautiful
to watch, marvels of Victorian design and mechanical
ability, put together from large iron castings exactingly
machined to be perfect for their purpose, and running

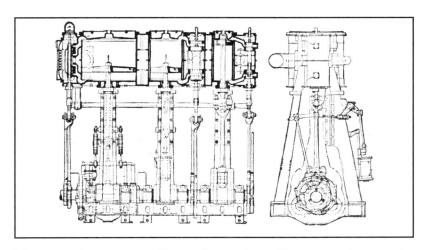

like very large complicated watches. Pistons, valves, rods, slides, cranks—all had to move in perfect and intricate harmony each with the other, with never a faltering, never a false move, and getting automatic squirts of oil in the proper places at the proper times. This was all orchestrated by the crank shaft and its cams; though the movements appeared impossibly complicated, false moves were actually impossible, for everything was cast and machined into the cold sparkling iron. The attendants, the Engine Room Artificers who looked after the engine, listened for any change in beat or rhythm, kept close watch on the oiling and on the flow of water and lubricants, and whether the bearings were overheating. On a reciprocating engine they tested for overheating by raising a hand and arm, getting it into motion synchronized with the motion of the part to be checked, and moving the hand in and out to touch the iron at the proper times. They were artists in their own right. If they found overheating on the bearings of the main engine, especially at high speed, it would be dealt with by throwing buckets of water onto the too-hot parts. LtCmdr Easton, Commanding Officer for a year in **HMCS *Baddeck***, has told us that all was not perfect in every one of these marvels of Victorian design and construction! In ***Baddeck*** he had endless trouble at sea with bearing problems and engine failures; he had to put up with it for almost a year before leaving the ship which he called "the bane of my recent life".

The engine room of a steam-driven corvette was not only a great sight; it had other qualities. The warmth arising from all the steam-heated parts, the odour of oil and machinery, the noise of the engine and other machinery working, the general feeling of order—all these gave one a perfect conviction that all was right with the world, and nothing could go wrong in such a place. The strongest of such feelings arose when manoeuvring. The telegraph from the bridge had been at Half (speed) Ahead for hours or even days. Came a ring for Slow Ahead, and the engine, responding to the turning of the throttle wheel, slowed down majestically. Then, perhaps, came Stop, then Half Astern, and the engine slowly decreased its complex motions until, briefly, they died out altogether. Then, with a sigh and in answer to the reversing gear, with utter languor the motion began in the reverse direction, turning the propeller in reverse and slowing the ship to a stop. Those, in fact, were usually the only engine orders received from the bridge in coming alongside a dock in **HMCS *Cobalt***. Judges was a master at such manoeuvring; the same could not be said for all captains! Of course, even in such an ordered environment things could indeed go wrong, and sometimes did, as Easton and his crew found. But such thoughts lay remote and unconsidered most of the time.

Special Hazards for Stokers and Engine Room Artificers

In a steam-driven ship, as in any other, the upper deck could be and often was a place of extreme discomfort, bitter cold, the blackness of night embracing it, sheets of sea water washing over it, and chaos in all the surrounding waters. At times of contact with enemy vessels, particularly at night, it was very evident that those vessels wished you no good as they sent off streams of painfully visible fire in your direction. The engine room by comparison was a place of pleasant comfort: warm, bright, cheerful, a place of peace, order, comforting sounds, and good behaviour, everything moving in its ordained manner. And from time to time on a watch there was KYE to brighten one's life—kye, a thick hot marvellous chocolate drink. All was indeed right with the world. Usually.

Usually!—though in the engine rooms and boiler rooms dangers lay all around. Foremost of the dangers was the fact of steam at very high pressure and temperature, confined in boilers and pipes everywhere. Those devices could burst from unfortunate failure or be burst by incoming shellfire, and then God help men in the spaces filled by the escaping steam. Escape from those spaces, if it was possible at all, meant climbing a long steep ladder from the very bottom of the ship to the only exit much higher up.

Though the danger from steam was real, it actually got very little thought. Of much more present and consuming concern at times was the question of what was going on above. Information came to the engine room from few sources—the telegraph which rang up orders from the bridge for the speed at which the engines were to turn, the voice pipe from the bridge down which a spooky voice would sometimes relay information, silences fraught with tension, and the noise of explosions both near and far. O yes—and also the motion of the deck underfoot. At times of a mighty tempest at sea that motion conveyed its own threat to all aboard when the ship lay over to the sea and seemed as though it would never right itself. In the machinery spaces the ladder, that life-saving exit to the open air, could then be impassable.

Strange happenings also could befall the "black gang" in dire times. In one serious grounding it happened that rock intruded itself through the ship's bottom skin, forcing up the deck plates in the boiler room. For the stokers such a sight was indeed terrifying. Earlier they had been able only to guess at strange happenings as the telegraph and voice pipe had announced extreme changes in the demand for steam. They had an even more precarious existence than the engine room crew, being in a much more cramped, noisy, hot and remote space. They too had but the one ladder for escape.

A major added danger in the boiler rooms was fire. When steaming at high speed the fires under a destroyer's boilers were very big, and action on the part of the stokers was needed to close them down—easy enough in normal times, but perhaps not in emergency conditions. Big fires in the wrong place can do big damage.

Many men were to be found below decks in time of war, in the machinery spaces and in other confined and lonely spaces within ships of war and in ships of commerce, men constrained to guessing about what was happening above, frightened. They and their shipmates above decks in the naval and the merchant services overcame their fears. In an important sense, they lived in a state of grace, and in that state kept the supply lines open despite the U-boats, thus ensuring that the profound evil of Naziism would find its nemesis in the Allied armies.

Steam presented another kind of threat to all on board. In the extreme, should a ship be sunk, the boilers, especially of the kind in *Cobalt*, could explode when suddenly immersed in cold water. Exploding boilers could be fatal for men in the water.

The Boiler Water Business

I was on board *Cobalt* to help the engine room staff learn how to look after the quality of the water in their boilers. To that end, on each watch they were instructed in the routines of taking a sample of the boiler water into a clean container, measuring out the proper amounts of it for analysis, putting it to the test with soap or silver solutions, keeping those solutions in proper condition, and maintaining the test log correctly for examination in Halifax. And above all, they were encouraged to find the methods easy and understandable and important.

Boilers produce steam, and it was steam that drove ships at sea for well over a hundred years, drove them faster and more reliably than sail had ever done. But the use of steam had a weak point that interfered with its true reliability—steam had to be made in boilers.

In the first days of steam at sea, early in the 1800s, boilers operated at very low pressure and the water which they turned into steam was straight simple sea water. Sea water contains salt in rather large amounts, and evaporation of steam from it soon results in the salt content being more than can remain dissolved. To avoid having the excess build up as solid material on iron surfaces where it would interfere with the passage of heat from the fire into the water, the boilers were emptied frequently, throwing away a lot of heat. Loss of useful heat at sea is not a Good Thing, for the amount of fuel a ship can carry limits the distance it can move under power, and engine/boiler designers worked hard to reduce all losses. By the early 1900s, this drive to reduce losses had resulted in boilers of much higher pressure and power, in which water of high quality had to be used. But still, water used in the boilers could not be perfect—it was made from sea water by distillation, and a small amount of sea water was inevitably mixed into the good water. The result was some continuing corrosion and scale formation in the boilers. Corrosion spelled the need for new boilers at some early time in the life of the ship, and scaling reduced the efficiency with which fuel was converted to steam for driving the ship. These problems were dealt with by shutting the boilers down from time to time for a good scrubbing out—for "boiler cleaning". The boilers in most corvettes were of the type called "Scotch Marine"—big hollow cylinders of iron, through which, from end to end, smaller tubes carried the hot gases from the burning fuel oil. Other kinds

NMM, number unknown (NU)

of ship had boilers in which the water passed through small tubes passing from a lower drum to an upper drum, with fire outside the tubes. Scale would form on the tube surfaces, and corrosion blisters would form here and there. Cleaning any boiler was not easy, being hot, dirty, dusty, and noisome work in cramped spaces. It was done by wire–brushing. The least enviable of all naval ratings were those engaged month in and month out on that tiring and miserable job. Those engaged in it were certainly amongst the Navy's unsung heroes.

Corvettes and other escort vessels by 1942 were pushed to and beyond the absolute ragged edge of endurance to deal with the power of the U–boat fleet, and sinkings in 1942 were frighteningly high in numbers. One important limitation on the escort vessels, almost all steam driven, was their need to remain in port for several days each month for the unavoidable boiler cleaning. The cleaning activity was great for the seagoing crews, often desperate in their need for rest, but it took up an important part of the fleet's active capabilities, reducing the number of ships at sea at any time A better way to deal with the corrosion and scaling lay at hand by proper treatment of the water, and in 1942-3 that better way moved to sea.

Naval Service Headquarters, having decided to go the route of Boiler Water treatment, took on Sam Baird, a chemical engineer, to head it all up, and R. Porter Bailey to preside over the Boiler Water office in Halifax. Oddly, Sam was in the Engineer Branch, wearing a purple stripe, and Porter was in the Special Branch, wearing a Green Stripe; all the other professional staff in the Boiler Water office were in the Engineer Branch—Alec Holden, Doug Hutton, Bill Dean, Jim Roxborough, Bob Walford. Roxborough had served at sea in the Mediterranean to earn his Watch-Keeper's Certificate, and that put him a cut above. The non-professional people in the office included LdgSto Hébert, who did the laborious jobs around the laboratory, but also knew much about the routines of Boiler Water treatment.

The dockyards of three ports, Halifax, Prince Rupert and Esquimalt, had offices for the management of water quality, Halifax being by far the biggest. These offices were charged with encouraging the engineer staff in all HM steam-driven ships to be interested in and to understand quality matters, helping them to keep a vigilant eye on quality through periodic testing, and supervising the effectiveness of their actions by inspection of records and inspection of the boilers themselves.

In HM Dockyard in Halifax, the warships were lined up six deep along the jetties and docks not far away from the boiler water office. One of the chores was inspection of boilers when they were cleaned. This involved finding at what dock the ship lay, going on board the ship (sometimes after having crossed the decks of several others closer to the dock), finding the Chief Engineer (sometimes a Petty Officer and sometimes a commissioned officer), putting on overalls, climbing into the boiler through a manhole, examining it from top to bottom for scale and corrosion, changing back into uniform with a white shirt, and writing a report when back in the office—a handwritten report, to be typed later. Our interests were in corrosion, mostly, which took various forms as scabs, pustules, gritty areas, shallow holes, pits, and so on. Bailey was interesting, in a limited way, totally devoted to his work, meticulous to a fault, insistent that every 'i' be dotted and every 't' crossed. He would allow no unusual statements in the reports. He read and reread and rewrote them all, and changed them into the style and wording he had decided on as proper for the Boiler Water office in HM Dockyard Halifax. Having been put into standard language, reports were typed, and filed in their proper place. Bureaucracy was well served. The staff gave Bailey a hard time in response to his meticulous adherence to some mystical standard of reporting, but youth and brashness often does that to elders. By mid-1943 the treatment program was already effective to an important extent, helped no doubt by Bailey's intense approach to the problems.

In the city of Halifax all the buildings needed paint, and had needed it for decades. The streets were narrow and unattractive, especially along Barrington Street toward HM Dockyard. The impressions of a stranger to Halifax, written about 1880, were interesting to read. Then, too, the stranger saw dirty and unpainted buildings, gloomy public buildings, a general mess. Fire was one of the great problems of the Halifax authorities. When the Fire Chief made recommendations about equipment for dealing with the problem, the 'experts' on Council did nothing except bicker and baulk, and nothing got done. Towards the outskirts, though, Halifax was an attractive city, with grass and trees before the houses, and paint on their walls.

The streetcars were a close approach to 'Toonerville Trolleys', a cartoon image of the 30s and 40s. Of the same design as the cars on Coxwell Avenue in Toronto, they had four wheels only, and were perhaps 30 ft long at most. The wheelbase was so short, in fact, that the whole vehicle rocked along, back and front ends pitching up and down in reverse concert, and enough to make one seasick. The cars were interesting in their progress as they went along, turned, turned, went along, turned, turned, turned, turned, went along, etc. They seemed to be routed to cover the whole downtown area in the fashion of a weaver's shuttle on a complex tapestry. The tracks being in terrible condition made the ride even more venturesome. But they had a saving grace, one that more than compensated for the physical discomfort. The drivers and staff were of the greatest help and super-polite. For strangers far from home, as were most matelots, they made life bearable.

A much smaller Boiler Water office was set up in Prince Rupert, with the author in charge. Getting to Prince Rupert in those days was a matter of taking the train to Vancouver, and the coastal steamer from there along the Coast. Both parts of the trip were of great interest. Ocean Falls had something like 130 inches of rain annually; it rained daily in torrents. The town was a paper mill town, built in a wilderness of trees and fiords, and the "roads" were of plank and posts. Prince Rupert had lots of rain too, mostly just a drizzle, not a real soaker, but almost daily. On those days when it didn't rain, the Naval base had a "make-and-mend"—the day off. Rain or no rain, though, the surroundings were intensely beautiful as fog and clouds hung around the tops of the mountains.

The Boiler Water office and laboratory in **HMCS Chatham** were on the dock, on the second floor of a two-story wooden building overlooking the harbour, the ships of His Majesty tied up just below the window. Out in the harbour, the salmon boats went put-putting past morning and night; they were "one-lungers", and really did put-put. The tides in Prince Rupert were phenomenal, ships rising and falling by more than twenty feet from high to low. This made going aboard or ashore quite interesting and risky at times.

In Prince Rupert, the Base Chief Engineer was Cmdr(E) Surtees. His reaction on meeting the new member of his staff, introduced by Sam Baird, was: "Well! What a waste of a good engineer. Engineer officers should be at sea, not cooped up ashore". And on he mumbled and commented. There was more of it from him in the early days of working for him, but it turned out he had a heart of gold. It helped that the Chief ERA in *Cobalt* was a former good shipmate of his. Because of that, Surtees took a liking to his new Boiler Water "expert"; when his assistant, Osborne, went on leave for Christmas, that totally inexperienced expert was appointed Assistant Base

Engineer Officer for the period. That didn't interfere with the Boiler Water business for there was little of it in Prince Rupert anyway.

Canada's naval presence at sea on the West Coast was made up of "minesweepers". Much smaller than corvettes, they were poorly suited to deep ocean work and had none of it in the Pacific. But their boilers got a good going over from the Boiler Water office. *Bellechasse*, *Chignecto*, *Miramichi*, *Outarde*, *Quatsino*, *Courtenay*, *Kelowna*—what a roster of names to make you shivery. Those responsible for deciding how Canadian ships should be named deserve a monument for they did indeed recite all of Canada from coast to coast. They were minesweepers but no mines were to be found on the West Coast, and their routine became to patrol the Dixon Inlet in pairs, going from side to side of the Inlet and back again. Very exciting! It was a grinding routine for the crews of those ships, punctuated by periods of other excitement in the big "city" of Prince Rupert. Also very rough at times. Sometimes they made a side trip to Juno, Alaska, and found the US crews very grateful for their presence; American ships were "dry", making rum or anything else spirited on board from a visiting Canadian ship enormously welcome. When D-Day came most of the West Coast minesweepers remained where they were; others, though, were collected into the English Channel and led the invasion forces, sweeping mines to ensure the safe passage of the troops behind them.

The ambience of Prince Rupert was there to be enjoyed to its full—fish boats, fish plants, totem poles, surrounding scenery, historic sites, interesting people and dress. The American army was also there, and responsible one night for an eerie experience. On the main street in the rain, local traffic was held up by an American military funeral. In the fog and rain and dark, by the light of very dim street lights, several hundred men went slipping noiselessly by on rubber soles and heels—a procession straight out of Edgar Allen Poe.

All was not rain and eeriness in Prince Rupert by any means! Those same Americans had a dandy system for bringing famous entertainers to their troops; when those entertainers came to their camp, the Canadians were invited to come along and enjoy the evening too. And so they all got to see and fall in love with Ingrid Bergman.

Some time in the late autumn, Hugh Macdonald, Lt, RCNVR, was married in the local church, and the newly-married pair was hurried through a canopy of raised sabres as they left the church. Hugh went from Prince Rupert to the Fleet Air Arm.

The shortness of useful activity in the Boiler Water office led to a letter of resignation which, of course, was not accepted. Complaints that there was insufficient to do at Prince Rupert eventually brought fruit, thanks no doubt to Surtees, and a transfer to **HMCS *Givenchy*** at Esquimalt in January of 1944.

Again there was little to do, but somehow it didn't last long; in February there were orders to join **HMCS *Qu'Appelle***, 'For Training'. That meant for exposure in the engine room until the Watch-Keeper's Certificate had been acquired, normally about six months. Surtees had a hand in this appointment, for his superior officer

Commander D.C. Wallace, RCNR,
Commanding Officer of HMCS CHATHAM
at Prince Rupert, from where he moved to
be QU'APPELLE's first commanding officer in
early 1944, and in June of that year to be
Executive Officer in the Canadian-crewed
aircraft carrier HMS PUNCHER RCN (NU)

at Rupert, Commander D. Wallace, had himself gone to **Qu'Appelle** as Commanding Officer not long before. Soon to be heard was the Bosun's pipe "Hands to Stations for leaving Harbour! Special sea-duty men close up!" The Bosun's pipe is one of the world's magic instruments, plaintive in its sound, far-reaching, and hallowed by centuries of use at sea. None who have heard it can forget.

The story is continued from the end of Chapter 1.

... Solomon's glass was at his eye;
The one-armed bosun alert stood by
And the fierce crew swarmed to the heaving rail,
Their eyes strained far to the dancing sail.
Then eager glances were thrown aloft;
The mad dwarf swung in the narrow croft
With the hatchet-point of his chin thrust out,
The brim of his black hat flopped about
By the clamorous breeze, and never his eyes
Were turned from the sail in its dancing rise. ...

The story is continued at the end of Chapter 3.

3. HMCS Qu'Appelle's Guns and Steam

Man cannot tell, but Allah knows
How much the other side was hurt!
"Boxing" R. Kipling

Her First Days in the RCN

HMCS Qu'Appelle, LIKE MANY OF HER CREW, came late to the strife. Commissioned in early 1944, she and her crew were indeed privileged to have their part in the destruction of the idea that drove Germany from 1933. By early 1944 the fullness of the threat to civilized society posed by the German U-boat had been controlled, in essence, and that manifestation of Germany's evil "National Socialist" idea had been countered by able Allied surface and air forces.

The first few weeks of **HMCS Qu'Appelle**'s existence in the RCN were crucially formative of the

morale and spirit on board the ship. Able Seaman Andy
Gillespie has written about it movingly and vividly
starting with the encouraging statement that "I joined
as part of what seemed at the time to be a press-gang
operation". He tells of being taken out of hospital in
Niobe as part of that operation, and goes on to describe
joining the ship at Kingston-upon-Hull, where she was
commissioned. After victualling and ammunitioning
they sailed for exercises at Tobermory, followed by a trip
to St John's. Then their troubles began. Says Gillespie:
"In company with **HMS *Vindex***, a small aircraft carrier,
west of the Azores connections had just been made
good for oiling one afternoon when ASDIC reported
two small echoes approaching the port side at high
speed. Two torpedo tracks were very visible between
our starboard side and ***Vindex***, and on our port side.
A grinding search brought no positive results.

"Hurricane! No words can adequately describe
the awesome power of weather at its worst. After a
fair spell of moderate to fine weather this monster
blew up in the middle of the night. All hands were
called to secure everything on the weather decks, and
to rig lifelines from the break of the fo'c'sle to the
after canopy. The first casualty was the small motor
boat, smashed to matchwood. Then came the pipe
'Man over the side!' The Buffer, checking security aft,
had been swept overboard. Despite the state of the sea
and the limitations it imposed on manoeuvring it was
possible to hold him in the big searchlight for over an
hour. But to no avail. Whenever the ship could close
on him, the sea simply swept him away, and eventually
he was lost to sight.

"Early the next morning George Miles was detailed to secure the scramble netting on the port side. As he approached the rail, a boarding sea picked him up and seemed to suck him right down; he was wearing a duffle coat and sea boots that couldn't be kicked off. His life jacket was one of the real old skimpy rubber belts, inflated by cartridge or by mouth, totally unreliable. George also was lost. I came around the side of the after canopy when a huge wave washed over the torpedo tubes, lifted me to the deckhead, and dumped me just inside the guardrail. Another maverick wave washed me and the EO partly under the guardrail and partly over the side. We were saved by the funnel stay. Many people were very badly banged about.

"With no one on deck and a minimal bridge staff the inclinometer went right off scale as the ship broached to, and lay for what seemed an eternity on her side. In the mess deck we were actually standing on the ship's side waiting for the order to abandon ship. It was remarkable—there was no panic, yet every man was aware of the certain death outside the hull. There were actually jokes being made about a big lad known as 'Tiny', as to whether he could fit through the escape hatch on which he stood, and about the said hatch being below the waterline. The order never came. The ship righted herself, and the weather moderated. We sailed into `Derry looking like a rag merchant's barrow. But we also carried another bizarre problem with us!

"Just after the hurricane many of us had become aware of a peculiar odour permeating the ship. Four men were found by the POs in an advanced state of intoxication in one of the messes. We knew they had been scrounging rum and conning the Supply PO out of some vanilla extract the previous day. Apparently this was not enough, leading one of them to slip into the Sick Bay and lift a can of ether. This they were drinking by the spoonful. Some of the POs managed to get them out of the way, and too much may not have been made of the affair, except for the discovery that the can of ether was the only one aboard. Of course there was an inquiry, but messdeck solidarity stonewalled things for about two weeks until one man who had a wife in Derry could stand it no longer and blew the whistle. It was a most unpleasant time indeed."

Indeed! The same events from an officer's view were written of years later by Lt Hank Dadson. Said he:

"It is true that it wasn't a particularly happy ship. We thought it was at first, but as we went along some troubles developed. To start with, as I remember it, I was the only officer with sea time in the previous six months, so it took time to work to a sea routine. The specialist officers were fresh from Navigation, ASDIC, and Torpedo Schools, but the main problem was 'drafting'.

"Being the last of several Canadian destroyers to commission through **HMCS** *Niobe* we found that as each earlier ship went through their workup they would draft back to Niobe all their 'Birds', who would then be redrafted to take the next ship to commission. So we accumulated a set of really bad ones. Unknown to the Captain and officers several leading hands set up a kind of Mafia on the mess decks, and held control through harassment and threats. The officers felt uneasy but couldn't put a finger on anything. There was a very unhappy seaman who wanted ashore so badly that he hid his dentures in a whaler, and reported the dentures lost at sea. The dentures were subsequently found, but the seaman was promised 'no defaulters' and a draft ashore if he would disclose the troubles forward.

"We immediately ordered 'Clear Lower Decks', and the officers moved in and searched every locker. We found piles of stolen property, both from ashore and Naval stores, but all this happened after the story which follows.

"Shortly after our workups were completed we were working out of Londonderry with an Escort Group of a small carrier (**HMS** *Vindex*) and frigates when a strong storm warning was put out. We were the only destroyer in the Group, and the Senior Officer, not wishing to ride out a storm with the limitations of a destroyer, detached us to return alone to Londonderry. The storm hit us late evening of the same day. The Buffer, doing rounds on the upper deck at 2100, was swept overboard; an immediate alarm was given, and a lifebuoy heaved over. The Buffer had on his new Canadian kapok life jacket with light and whistle, and strong rescue attempts were made over the next

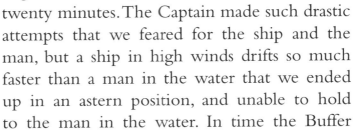

twenty minutes. The Captain made such drastic attempts that we feared for the ship and the man, but a ship in high winds drifts so much faster than a man in the water that we ended up in an astern position, and unable to hold to the man in the water. In time the Buffer went unconscious, and the gap widened to 'No Contact'. He was in sight by his light and blowing his whistle throughout the attempt up to that point. At 0700, volunteers were called for to clear the lines and scrambling nets on the upper decks and over the side, and it was during this operation that the second man, a volunteer, was lost over the side. He had high sea boots on and never came to the surface. ...

"It was during this trip that the bad group below deck broke into Sick Bay and stole alcohol, ether, etc. to make a brew in the mess decks. The result was that we had two Courts of Enquiry going simultaneously when we returned to Londonderry."

For that time there is in the National Archives today a 'List of Men Under Punishment'.

Not long afterwards all had greatly improved, and only veiled references were to be heard to the losses at sea earlier and to the unpleasantness with some of the crew, but never could one get a straight story until years later.

The Ship

Her Class

HMCS *Qu'Appelle* was commissioned into the Royal Canadian Navy on 8th February of 1944. She had been in the Royal Navy since 1934 when she was launched, as **HMS *Foxhound***, and had had close–in action in Norway, the Far East, and the Mediterranean. She and her sister ship ***Firedrake*** were responsible for the first sinking of a U-boat (U 39), 14 September,

1939, very early in the war. At the time of her transfer to us, she had steamed more miles than any other warship in the Allied navies—280,000 of them, most of those as part of the famous 'Force H', about which much has been written. In the Royal Navy she was one of a number of F–Class destroyers. Renamed on commissioning into the Canadian Navy, her class name was also changed, to River Class. Others of her class included **Restigouche**, **Saguenay**, **Saskatchewan**, **Skeena**, **Gatineau**, **Ottawa**, **Kootenay**, **Chaudiere**, **Margaree**, **Assiniboine**, **St Laurent**, and **Fraser**. With half of these we were closely involved in the months to come, but the only similarity between them, apart from being destroyers, was that they had the names of Canadian rivers. (They are all great Canadian names, and like other names of RCN ships charged full of Canada.) Two of the River Class Destroyers were actually built for Canada in England (**Skeena** and **Saguenay**), but **Qu'Appelle** was not; she was the last of the class transferred from the RN. **Qu'Appelle** also differed from the other River Class ships in having been built with more accommodation for officers, allowing her therefore to perform as leader or Senior Officer of any group she might be in. Lead ships had to carry people to manage the group as well as those who managed the ship itself.

Destroyers, as a type of warship, had been invented and developed in the 1890s in response to another type of warship called a torpedo boat. The torpedo boat was armed with the newfangled torpedo and was considered a terrible threat to battleships, then the real backbone and strength of a fleet. Something had to be done, and intense effort went into designing and building a vessel that would catch and destroy the torpedo boats. One of the major accomplishments of the time was to get the speed up, for no ship could catch a torpedo boat if it couldn't go faster than its prey. After a few years, it was realized that the type of vessel that had been developed could be both a catcher of torpedo boats and itself a torpedo-carrying ship, and the two types became one with the type-name "torpedo boat destroyers".

Though still called destroyers, armament in Canada's River Class ships had been radically changed in the course of the first years of the war as anti-submarine activity became an absolute priority. Of **Foxhound**'s four 4.7 inch guns, one had been removed to make room for depth charges on the after deck and another for Hedgehog on the fore deck, and four of her eight torpedoes had also been removed. She was, in fact, converted into a vessel suited strictly only for anti–submarine action, differing from the smaller and more numerous A/S vessels like corvettes in her size, speed, and unimportant aspects of armament. She could move at almost 30 knots. When new from her builders' hands she had even more speed, but age and the weight of additional armament and other gear slowed her down in later life.

The Ship's Badge

Somewhat of a romantic when it came to the Navy and the ships he served in, the Engineer Officer in the later months of 1944 had arranged by 'pulling strings and cashing chips' for the approval of a ship's badge,

and for its casting in aluminum. The shape of the frame for the badge is that adopted in 1919 by the RN for destroyers, but somehow those who designed the badge in 1945 did not know that the Admiralty had changed shapes during the war, and all vessels were to have circular frames. The same policy was adopted in Canada in 1946—the year in which *Qu'Appelle* was removed from service. Who designed or approved the 1944 badge was never learned.

The actual official badge for *Qu'Appelle* is given in *Arbuckle* (Nimbus Publishing, 1984). The official explanation of the heraldic design attributes the whole fox motif to the idea of 'an intent listening and watching'. The fox's head is actually reminiscent of the ship's earlier history as HMS *Foxhound*, making a nice continuity with its former days and with the one-time close relationships with the RN.

Her Boilers

Driving *Qu'Appelle* were two screws, turning at a maximum of about 350 revolutions a minute (revs), and powered by two steam turbine engines of about 16,000 HP each. The steam came from three water-tube boilers, at a maximum pressure of about 325 pounds per square inch, and superheated to 700° F. Water-tube boilers have the water inside small tubes that connect upper and lower drums containing water, the fire being outside the tubes, a big fire. Each of these boilers, when running at full speed, had to produce over 2,000 pounds of steam a minute. That much steam required an inferno of fire under each boiler, produced by nine oil burners—over 15 gallons of fuel got burned every minute. Furthermore, the amount of water in the boiler was small, and it could disappear out of the gauge glasses in a twinkling. Loss of water would result in the boiler tubes overheating and burning out, and so was very serious. Running such boilers was no sinecure for the Stokers involved.

NMM 30025

When the ship was being manoeuvred with many wide changes in speed the three men in each boiler room had to be wizards to keep up. When the revs dropped from Full to Slow the amount of steam needed by the engines decreased suddenly to a tenth of its initial amount. Then the Stokers had to shut off fires quickly, watch the gauge glasses, watch the fuel pumps, and slow down air fans, all in a few seconds. (They had to watch gauge glasses in **Qu'Appelle** because the automatic water-level controllers didn't work well, and couldn't be relied on, adding substantially to the pressures and worries besetting the stokehold crews.)

Each boiler was in its own cramped boiler space, about 25 ft long, and the full width of the ship. Air in each boiler room was pressurized by big fans, and getting out of the rooms meant climbing a ladder to an air lock, a small space with two doors, only one of which could be open at a time; while in the air lock, one door led to the boiler room, the other to the main deck. It was the only exit.

Her Engine Room

As seen in the sketches on the next page, the engine room space, about 52 ft long, was reached only by way of the access hatches and two ladders almost side by side; the bulkheads fore and aft allowed of no access through them. Forward of the engine room was No. 3 boiler room, with two more forward of that again, each with its own bulkheads. Aft of the engine room was a cabin flat, with four cabins, two to each side, below which were fuel oil tanks. Aft again of that cabin flat was the wardroom flat, with some more officers'

HMS *Inglefield, similar to **HMCS *Qu'Appelle** (EX **HMS *Foxhound*)
NMM 15410

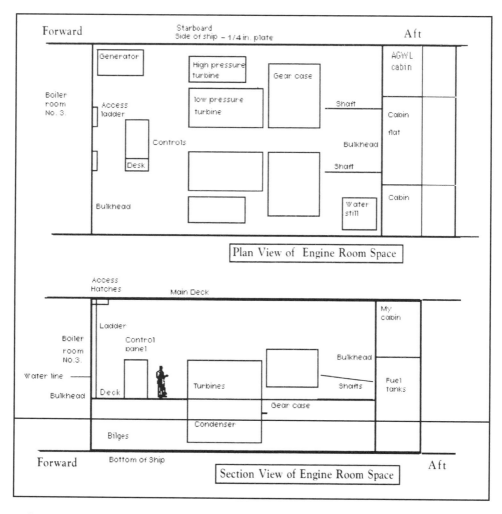

Plan View of Engine Room Space

Section View of Engine Room Space

cabins, the wardroom galley, and the wardroom itself.

In talking of **Cobalt**, the point was made that a steam engine could be made big and slow or small and fast for a given power output. The designers of turbines, engines like those in **Qu'Appelle**, chose the small and fast approach, so making the engines much smaller, though more powerful than those in corvettes, but necessitating speed reduction between engine and propeller.

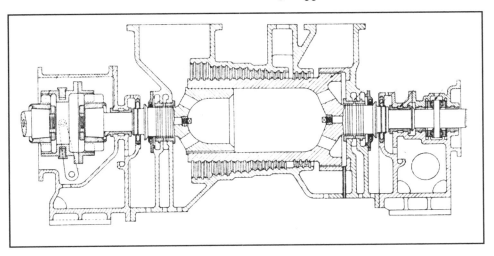

Those designers were approaching the end of the days of steam. "Glo———r—i—ous steam", said the chapter about *Cobalt*. It was not glorious at all for many members of engine and boiler room crews. Made in boilers and carried in big pipes that were vulnerable to shot and shell, steam could escape from a burst pipe or boiler at high temperature and high velocity, scalding and burning and suffocating all in its path or vicinity. Later vessels used diesel engines, in which the fuel is burned directly in the engine cylinders, so avoiding altogether the need for the dangers of steam. (Diesels also are big and slow—later vessels again used turbines in a small and fast approach, but a kind of turbine in which also fuel could be burned directly. The latter arose out of the aircraft industry, in which in 1944 Sir Frank Whittle of the RAF was showing what his jet engines—turbines—could do). The days of the dominance of steam at sea were soon to come to an end!

Qu'Appelle's two engines were each made up of two units, the first taking high-pressure steam, followed by a low-pressure unit. Steam came to the high-pressure units from the boiler rooms past shut-off valves and a throttle valve which was used to control the speed at which they turned. Expanding through the high-pressure units, the steam then went to the low-pressure turbines, and out of them to the condensers to be returned to the liquid state for use again in the boilers. Since the turbines turned at very high speed (3,300 revolutions per minute in the HP units, and 2,200 in the LP units), and the screws driving the ship had to turn at slow speed (350 "revs" maximum), there were very large gear-reducers between the engines and the shafts carrying the screws. These shafts were big, around twelve inches in diameter, and ran through the stern tube to the outside of the vessel.

There was much more in the engine room. The ship had to be provided with electrical power, generated in the engine room, and controlled with electrical control panels. Water had to be made from seawater, for shipboard use and for the boilers, in evaporators heated by steam. Seawater had to be pumped to various pipelines for washing down decks and for fire-fighting. The engines themselves required various services, of lubricating oil, of condenser cooling water, of air removal pumps. Most of these services were provided by steam-driven machinery, and in total between the boiler rooms and the engine room, there were almost three dozen turbines in use as drivers on the service machinery

But at times, more important than all that, was a little steam outlet beside the desk. On a long night watch, the call would come for Kye. Into a pot would go a big block of coarse chocolate, some sugar, some condensed milk, some water ... and open steam. Zzzzzzzz it would go, the pitch rising as the contents heated up, just like some of today's machines for making cafe-au-lait. And out of the pot into mugs we poured the richest, thickest ambrosial hot chocolate imaginable. It is probably better in retrospect than the reality justified—but nothing else could have approached its magic in raising flagging spirits on watch in the small hours of the morning. Kye was a Royal Navy tradition, starting about 1835. The Kye was made by the forward side of the desk, behind the control panel. On the desk we kept the log of engine room operations, particularly of orders from the bridge, but at the right time all was subordinate to Kye.

Orders for speed came at times by telegraph, a dial on the control panel which was activated from the bridge, a bell ringing as the bridge made an order. The order was acknowledged by moving a lever on the dial, and entered in the log. Speed orders also at times called for a specific rotation rate for the propellers. The engine speed was then set at the required level by means of a control wheel at the panel, which changed the pressure of steam allowed into the high-pressure turbine. There was one control for each engine.

I have already waxed somewhat lyrical about the complex dance of the parts of the reciprocating engine in **HMCS** *Cobalt*, with all its Victorian ingenuity and mechanical craftsmanship. A steam turbine engine has no open display of such ingenuity or elegance, no brass parts to keep shined up, no cranks with which to synchronize one's arm and hand to test bearing temperature. But inside it and its gear reducers, it is a marvel of the skills of man, developed in late Victorian times and thereafter honed to a pitch of excellence and perfection.

The drawing on page 45 shows a section through a steam turbine engine; the photograph to the right is of the rotor of **HMS** *Fortune* (later **HMCS** *Saskatchewan*, a sister ship of *Qu'Appelle*), the top casing having been removed from the engine for repairs soon

NMM 67191

after the ship was launched. The reason for the need for repairs can be seen in the photograph; some of the blades had been damaged, probably by a small piece of steel left loose in the casing on assembly. The rings of blades shown on the rotor fit closely between similar fixed blades. Steam from the nozzles is directed against the first row of rotor blades, leaves them and is redirected by the fixed blades to enter the second row of rotor blades, pushing against all rotor blades as it moves and expands from inlet end to outlet end of the engine. Some of the men who built the engines in *Qu'Appelle* were apprentices when the development of the steam turbine had just started.

The Ship's Book

There is, in the National Archives in Ottawa, in Record Group 24, Volume 6093, a document called the Ship's Book. When **HMS** *Foxhound* was commissioned in 1935, the Ship's Book was started, and it was kept current until the day she was recommissioned as **HMCS** *Qu'Appelle*. The book is a great leather bound scrapbook, into which documents dealing with the ship could be fastened. And they were, in their bewildering complexity. The Royal Navy was meticulous, especially in peacetime, in its record keeping. In the book, in the most carefully entered forms, are the records of the hull, the engines, the armament, the inclining tests, the speed trials, the dry-dockings year by year for inspection and bottom coating, the machinery conditions, the boiler tube status, and on and on, each record attested by the proper official signatures, and stamps, and seals. There we find that the propellers were 9 feet 10 inches in diameter at their tips, that the ship was all of ¼ inch longer as built than the drawings provided for, that the capacity for making fresh water was 50 tons daily. It is all fascinating reading, ending abruptly with the single page, signed by the ship's new Canadian officers, acknowledging her refit completed on the day she was recommissioned. Ah me, so pass all human artifacts. The Ship's Book will languish in the Archives for a hundred years, maybe five, the leather mouldering, and the pages sticking together (some of them do so now, a bit!), eventually to return to dust, joining the ship herself in the realm of things totally forgotten.

SPEED	OIL USED	ENDURANCE	RANGE	GO!
knots	tons daily	days	miles	Feet covered per gallon of oil burned
6	14.4	32.6	4700	264
8	17.0	27.6	5308	298
10	20.0	23.5	5640	317
12	24.2	19.4	5593	314
14	29.7	15.8	5317	299
16	40.1	11.7	4501	253
18	53.5	8.8	3795	213
20	69.6	6.8	3241	182
22	89.5	5.3	2773	156
24	106.8	4.4	2535	142
26	130.0	3.6	2256	127
28	156.0	3.0	2025	114
30	200.0	2.4	1692	95
32	256.1	1.8	1409	79
33	293.5	1.6	1268	71

Speed and Fuel Consumption

One of the things given in the Ship's Book is the record of the Fuel Economy trials carried out in 1935. At that time the ship didn't have on board all the equipment and men that she carried in wartime, and then she made just over 33 knots with tanks half full. The record is interesting.

The miles per gallon was not very much, so little in fact that it is given here as *feet* per gallon! It was obviously highly dependent on the speed, and there was a speed, the "cruising speed", that produced the most feet per gallon. In actual fact **Qu'Appelle** had no opportunity to produce its own record of endurance at various speeds, and used one from **Saskatchewan**. The Engineer Officer had to concern himself continually with these numbers and considerations, as he had to report to the Captain daily the state of the fuel reserves and the furthest the ship could go before refuelling. Each day at sea the Chief Stoker sounded the tanks, determining how much oil remained on board, and reported the result to the Chief Engineer. If it were reported to him that the remaining fuel amounted to, say, 121 tons, and the ship was making a current speed of 20 knots, he could report to the Captain that the remaining 121 tons of fuel was good for 121/69.6 or 1.74 days of steaming at the current speed (just over 41 hours), or a distance of just over 41 × 20 or 820 miles. At the most economical speed the distance could be extended to 1,430 miles. If the actual distance to a fuelling port were more than those 1,430 miles, then refuelling at sea would obviously be necessary.

The amount of fuel remaining in the tanks was one of a Commanding Officer's primary concerns, uppermost in his mind and worries when contact was being sought with an elusive enemy. A classical case of such concerns and their influence on the battle occurred during the pursuit of the German battleship **Bismark**.

Her Organization

A ship of war is made up of the animate and the inanimate, and possibly the most important part of the inanimate is her organization, the system which ensures that everyone works as part of a team (or at least has that objective as an ideal; the animate part, her people, are not ideal, and sometimes don't cooperate with the other part nor with each other very well). The people were organized into three watches, Red, White, and Blue, a long-established system that recognized the basic desirability of eight hour days. Every man of the crew was assigned to a watch and detailed to certain jobs specific to whether the ship was at Cruising, Defence, or Action Stations.

A further set of divisions of responsibilities had to do with areas of special ability or expertise. In days gone, those days of wooden ships, the basic division of expertise was into seamen, who ran the ship, and marines who fought it and imposed discipline. Mechanization and technology added many more divisions, called Branches, and changed the structure profoundly. Now there were Seamen (who looked after many of the things on deck—guns, ASDIC, radar, and general seamanship duties); Torpedo hands (who looked after electrical matters and the torpedoes); Communications hands (for visual and radio signalling); Supply hands (who served as cooks and stewards); and the Engine Room and Stoker crews. The head rating in each branch was the Chief Petty Officer or a Petty Officer. These senior people had their own quarters and mess. The ratings messed in groups of about ten, mostly all of a Branch, in charge of a Leading hand, who distributed the rations collected by a messman from the galley.

In those days a centuries-old tradition of the Royal Navy was still in effect in the Canadian service—the issue of rum once a day, under the control of the Coxswain, and following the pipe "Up Spirits!" The rum was not today's 40% alcohol of the Liquor Control Boards or something now called, erroneously, Pusser's Rum, but a far stronger thing. Men saved it up in bottles (strictly illegal, according to King's Regulations and Admiralty Instructions!), treasuring it, and used it as a currency for special favours from others, giving Sippers, and Gulpers, and other rewards.

It was men who made the ship a ship, and organization that made that possible for them. Of those men, some of them to be categorized as "Great", there will be more to say.

First sight of Ireland

My first sight of Ireland came in late April of 1944. Halifax in the spring was a place of slush and water on the streets, and a lot of walking would bring on wet feet, a fact that could cause subsequent trouble. To one given to colds and tonsillitis at the best of times, having such wet and cold feet gave those calamities a perfect opening, and they struck with vengeance pretty soon.

But before they did, with their full fury, I had joined the minesweeper **HMCS *Drummondville*** for passage to St John's, Newfoundland, there to join **HMCS *Qu'Appelle***. The full fury of illness arrived within a day, and I found myself confined to my bunk, unable to eat anything for the swelling of my throat. One of the Petty Officers nursed me, brought me juices to drink, and watched over me. I was in serious condition, and still not recovered to normal on arrival in St John's a week or so later.

Arrived, I reported to my new ship, there to meet the doctor, Max Frost, Lt(S), RCNVR. Max was loath to allow me to join, but sent me to the hospital for checkup, and there I got the green light, provided Max

would accept me. He
did, fortunately. So off
I went, now Senior
Engineer in **HMCS**
Qu'Appelle. "Senior
Engineer" was not a
naval designation, but

one adopted from the merchant service to apply to
the Chief Engineer's assistant. My objective in that
position was to earn the Watch-Keeping Certificate,
which would attest to a presumed competence to
manage the engineering department of a ship of war.

Midway across the North Atlantic, we had some
kind of problem with the Hele-Shaw steering engine,
and came to a full dead stop amidst the submarines
while the steering engine was dismantled, repaired, and
reassembled. Being in the tiller flat, dead in the water,
with the steering engine in parts all around us, waiting
with one side of our being all tensed up for attention
from a passing U-boat, was an eerie experience, but
a very good one for the fresh-faced Senior Engineer,
totally new to the sea. Getting the engine going again
took a few hours, then we steamed off to Londonderry,
safe and sound still.

A week out of St John's, recovery almost complete,
Ireland was close. She came into view slowly, a hazy
line on the horizon first, a line that grew and grew
and became the most beautiful of sights, the sun
dappling the emerald green countryside, the fields
lying in helter-skelter order, threadlike roads running
jiggly here and there. But the greens! Many a Canadian
coming in from sea must have had the same impression,

for here is how Curry describes it in his book—

"We were now ready for our first glimpse of Paradise. … We were surrounded on both sides with the utter beauty of green Ireland, and it was as if the fairies themselves had wafted us into a land of magic that was almost beyond belief. Loch Foyle was so narrow all the way into Derry that we felt we could almost reach out and touch this beautiful land—peaceful, gentle, and lush."

Especially, though, for someone who had thought himself at the point of death, first from tonsillitis, then from a faulty steering engine, it was an unforgettable sight.

Chief Engineer Palmer

The Man

I.J.L. Palmer was Chief Engineer of **HMCS** *Qu'Appelle* from April on, succeeding the first to hold the position. The first name was Ivor, but he

was known by the second, Jim, except on board ship, where he was "Chief" usually, or Mr Palmer. About 35 years of age, slight, fair complexioned, and a LtCmdr, RCNR, he took

LtCmdr. I.J.L. Palmer, RCNR, at work in August, 1944, on his most-used tool (for lengthy lists of alterations, additions, repairs, and the like). The official photographer has placed him at the wardroom table, and behind can be seen the wardroom notice board, and the hatch through to the galley. RCN A986

his duties seriously. The only part of his seagoing experience which he spoke of, and then only briefly, was in **HMCS *Prince Robert***, which he had left to join *Qu'Appelle*. He was definitely very likeable, and a very good teacher. The ratings of the Engineering Department did not all agree with these views, thinking him cold and remote. StoPO George Stone, for example, had been in seagoing vessels for over 1,500 days, and thought he should have some relief from such activities! He was abruptly turned down by the Chief Engineer, and retained some bitterness over the fact. Palmer, however, was not about to let go of any of his best people whether they liked it or not.

But he did have his very human qualities and they were recognized. One day the stokers coming on watch brought with them a bucket of potatoes. They were put in the hp nozzle control boxes on the turbines. In an hour and a half, voilá! Baked potatoes. Then, surprisingly, a messenger was sent to ask Palmer if he would like some for his dinner. He was extremely pleased, and enjoyed the double blessing, very tasty potatoes and an unexpected vote of confidence from his crew.

Walks in the Country

As occasion offered, Palmer and his Senior Engineer walked in the British countryside, out of Londonderry or out of Plymouth. A great feature of British towns in those days was the nearness of country to city; one could walk completely out of the town in little time. From Jim Palmer for the first hour there was nothing but talk of the ship, or of the other officers, or of the

Chief Engine Room Artificer, with whom he didn't get on well at all. After an hour of near-continuous monologue on these subjects, he began to notice nature around him, and to appreciate it, commenting on the flowers, the fields, the road, the buildings, the animals. Then silence pervaded him, and nothing could pry a word out. I have elsewhere referred to the somewhat amateur nature of some of my RCN confrères. The comment does not apply to I.J.L. Palmer, a true RCNR professional! His concentration on talk about the ship during our walks was a demonstration of his intense absorption in his work, and fretful worry about his responsibilities.

The Chief Engineer's Duties and Routines

Still preserved is a letter that the Chief wrote when he had to go to hospital for a period in mid-August of 1944. Ever mindful of his duties and the ship, he wrote instructions that his assistant was to have on return from leave. Here they are:

"I am writing you this in case you have not returned by the time I leave for hospital; Doc can tell you all about it. It may be a week or it may be three weeks before I am back on my feet again. I have really suffered plenty of pain during the past week, and being tied down on board after the long spell at sea has not improved things with the monotony of life on board in dry dock.

"These are just a few words of advice in case you have to take her out by yourself.

"Before leaving always try out all the gear, you go up to the bridge and try out the sirens, telegraphs, and revolution indicators yourself; have the Chief ERA go to the tiller flat and watch the steering gear while you turn the wheel from port to starboard. NB.— You close the Bypass on the pedestal yourself before trying the wheel, push down the handle and screw in the pin tight. Try the wheel hard over from Port to Starboard first of all, then back to 30 degrees Port to 25 degrees Starboard, then back to 20 degrees to Port to 15 degrees Starboard, and so on till you finally get back to mid–ships. Then try out the main engines after telling the officer of the watch or day. When all is tried out report to the Captain about ten minutes before slipping time.

"Each evening at sea, the CERA should report 'Rounds Correct' sometime between 1930 and 2030. It is good practice to take a look at the steering gear yourself, then take a look in the engine room, and report Engineer's Rounds Correct to the Captain about 2100. If he was asleep, I never woke him up, but asked the Officer of the Watch to let him know I had been up when he woke.

"In connection with the running, I would run the job just like I ran her as regards nozzles, fuel, etc. Put your foot down if any attempt is made to change the routine about these; you know the story about fuel consumption before I came here (the shore authorities found it unacceptably high—AGWL), and so I would advise keeping as close as possible to the routine we have had here (which was to shut off many of the nozzles in the engines—AGWL). Keep your eye on your fuel, it is the biggest worry of all. Remember too that the evaporator consumption after nine or ten days' use is such that it is profitable to change the coils;

now with the shortage of men, try to do it when in port. If the Chief ERA quibbles about it put your foot down. I may as well tell you that in his last ship he tried to run the young chap there and apparently got away with it.

"The best temperature for the main fridge is around 17 to say 26 degrees; last trip I instituted the practice of getting the temperatures each day and entering them in the register. The Chief Stoker takes the fuel tanks each morning and sends a chit to the bridge. It is best to use one boiler for'd and one aft. He is good at it now; however, always try to empty the aft tanks first, the for'd keeps her nose down at high speeds. Also try to keep as much of your residue as possible in one set of tanks, i.e., drain all the others dry. The idea in for'd and aft should definitely always be the rule in action in case damage should arise. Keep some water in the starb'd peace tank in No.2 boiler room; this ship has a port list and that is the only way to keep her upright. NOTE: No fuel is carried in the Peace tanks by order of the authorities in Londonderry; I mention this in case there is a new CO, and he may want to know why they are empty.

"There is a typewritten sheet from **EO** *Saskatchewan* re his consumptions which is pretty good for us also, besides the sheet that is at the right hand end of the bookshelf.

"Should fortune so decree and I do not return and you go home to Canada, do not forget to have a signal sent to COM(D) Londonderry (R) EOR requesting that spare gear may be forwarded to Moville if you did not go to Londonderry itself; if you do go, well just contact Lt Bird.

"In Plymouth this time after I put in the first defect list I put in the remainder by signal. You get better results. If you are stuck, go and see Mr. Parker or Mr. Dawe—keep away from McGill; he is not so hot, always full of work somewhere else. The following are good phone numbers to remember (follows a list, with inspectors, foremen, chargemen, offices).

"They will not do any work in the Machine Shops without a Pink Slip from Mr. Dawe or Mr. Parker. Look at my signal pad for old signals for routine to be carried out. If I am not back for a while, and you come into Plymouth and have any defects, go up in the first instance and see the Engineer Commander himself. Do not pay attention to the others around. He alone can sanction anything, and even then it is necessary to see the various chaps I have mentioned above; if you do not go and see them you find time flies and no one comes around to see you.

"There are two funnel covers on order, and will find out about them at phone 691. We have cleaned the boilers externally, so count your hours from zero when you leave. Any ship in Plymouth for five days must boiler clean."

The letter is quoted at length, for it says so much about a great Chief Engineer, as well as about his worries. The letter says little about the engine room itself, but dwells on the two primary preoccupations of a Chief Engineer—fuel and repairs. Of all the people aboard, it is he who carries the most burdensome responsibility. Of course one must recognize clearly the lonely responsibility of the commanding officer, the

Captain. But the Engineer Officer knows intimately the physical weak points in the ship and its ability to continue moving at sea, and they are his responsibility. To keep moving at sea is of first importance in time of war, for the stopped vessel is a prime target for attack, let alone being uselessly unable to fulfil her role and purpose. Chief Engineer Palmer was acutely aware of this responsibility, and it weighed on him.

One cross that Palmer had to bear was the Chief Engine Room Artificer, the engine room rating who corresponded to Chief Stoker Patry in the Stoker Department. It was he to whom Palmer gave orders affecting the engine room. And he was not a cooperative individual, but one who bucked and resisted (and resented?) what he was ordered to do. The Chief ERA was obviously an experienced and able man, but also obvious was the personality conflict between him and Palmer. I had little to do with him—but anticipating that I would, and worrying about it, Palmer included him in the letter. The efficient working of people together was also one of his responsibilities, and a big one.

In the event, he came back from the hospital in time, and stayed with the ship. As a footnote, there was no possibility that I could in fact have "taken her out", for to do so required the Watch-Keeper's Certificate, let alone far more experience than I had gathered; the Captain could certainly not entrust his ship and his crew to anyone in my position. For the Certificate, I had still two months to go; for experience adequate to managing a destroyer's engineering matters, years would have had to pass!

The Ship in Port

A ship is intended to be at sea, and at sea is at its most noble and exciting. But being at sea is not possible for 100% of the time—it is necessary to be in harbour at times. Life on board was bedlam in harbour. In some ways it provided the most varied life for crew and ship, with the untidiness of repairs and work crews on the one hand, and the tidiness set up in some parts on the other hand for parties or inspections. Every time in port did not see a party in the Wardroom, but sometimes there was one. They were happy and pleasant diversions, especially when they brought aboard various nurses and other female persons—or so thought most of the officers and crew. The crew had a rather prejudiced view of those parties, as is evident from the pictorial report in the ship's newsletter!

On business hours in port, Jim took his Assistant around with him to the various dockyard offices, dickering for repairs, additions, stores, boiler cleaning. The last days at sea were periods when Palmer sat endlessly at the old typewriter in his cabin, preparing the paperwork required to support all these

dockyard visits, and spending a lot of time with the Captain going over them. In port during some of these times, the relatively immaculate engine room became a disaster area, with dockyard hands all over the place. It seemed at times that they spent more time preparing and drinking tea than they did working, especially in Plymouth! In fact, the whole ship was a distinctly different and an almost-unpleasantly-unfamiliar thing at times in port if there was much work to do. One of those times was after we were struck by **Skeena**, and had to be dry-docked for repairs. It was interesting to see the bottom of the ship, but apart from that, she was like a dead thing in port.

Londonderry and Plymouth

Londonderry was the principal base for Canadian warships on the eastern side of the Atlantic, and

there you would find corvettes side by side at the docks, just as at Halifax on the other side of the ocean. When we were in Londonderry Jim took me of a Sunday afternoon to visit an Irish family he had got to know, and there we had tea and cakes. There were numerous friendly liaisons between the Navy and the Londonderry folk, liaisons that were important in making life again acceptable for men who spent long bitter times at sea, and it was a privilege to be introduced to some of that friendliness. Londonderry had had almost none of the unhappy aspects of war visited on it, and in that differed widely from Plymouth.

Plymouth was one of the staging ports in the south of England for the invasion of Europe, and in mid-1944 was full of vessels preparing for that onslaught. Physically, Plymouth was a mess, a mess left over from the blitz of earlier years. Blocks of buildings had been felled, blocks of houses stood roofless, there were gaps everywhere in the rows of houses, lifeless homes, glassless windows, isolated fireplaces, twisted bedsteads in the rubble, a shell of stone left of the Cathedral. Those who stayed in the city and lived through the days of bombing obviously were full of stubborn courage and plain guts. The people of Plymouth were not alone in exhibiting such qualities, and as everywhere that disaster strikes hard life went on cheerfully and busily.

Spare Parts

When we left Londonderry for Plymouth, I was assigned a chore that occupied me at sea for some weeks. You will recall that much of the Chief's letter when he was leaving for the hospital dealt with repairs. Much of his time at sea was occupied in preparing lists of A & As (alterations and additions) needed, and lists of repairs that must be done when we arrived again in port. Then in port he had to hassle all the time with the shore authorities to get the work done. Whether ashore or afloat, repairs to machinery are greatly simplified if a part of the machine can be taken out of some store, so avoiding the need to be made anew every time it is needed. Those parts in the store are called "Spare Parts". Immediate access to Spare Parts was extremely important to a ship in our situation, for most of them were of a special nature, difficult to replace either by purchase or by special manufacture. In **Qu'Appelle**, the Spare Parts' situation was in poor shape, with lots of parts around the ship, but no adequate record of what or where. Overall, then, Spare Parts loomed large.

It was my task to find everything, by crawling through all the obscure spaces I could find, poking around for the parts, then listing them by number and name. Many of the parts were quite large, and most of these large ones were fastened to bulkheads, the ship's side, and other surfaces, wherever was convenient, by steel clips. So there was the Senior Engineer, weather or no, the beaches of Normandy not far away, in any moments not otherwise occupied, crawling through any and all unlikely spaces, identifying and listing parts, serial numbers, locations, etc. **Qu'Appelle** came to have the most complete list of parts in the whole of the Naval service!

I also had to get to know the various pipe runs and valve locations, sketching them and memorizing them. Following pipe runs and finding spare parts at sea is not everyone's idea of a good time, and weak stomachs would not be able to do it.

Watch Keeping

The organization of the Spare Parts' situation on board the ship was to occupy all off-watch time for weeks. It was normal at sea to stand watch, and everyone did so except the Captain, the Chief Engineer, and certain specialists in the crew. (It is interesting that, in the days of sail and wooden ships, those who did not stand watch were called "idlers". The meaning of the word has changed since those days!) Standing watch meant four hours on then eight off, except when the Dog Watches came around. There were two Dogs, each of two hours, from 1600 to 2000; their purpose was to cause a rotation of times on watch, and to allow time for the evening meal. The hours off in the daytime were not playtime. The hands were organized into working parties, and chipped paint, or did whatever else was required. The officers had their own chores in the way of paperwork, supervising the work, etc. And I had the Spare Parts.

Watch keeping in the machinery spaces presented its problems in the way of clothes.

The author, sitting in the X-gun mount, in the Irish sea, another of HMC ships in the background. Note the gadget in hand – the "life-vest" carried by a large number of Canadians at sea, even as late as 1944, before proper jackets had been issued to all. It is a rubber ring, blown up by mouth through a tube. That so many in the Canadian Naval Service were sent to sea with such inadequate life-jackets is a disgrace; many lost lives must be attributed to it.

Most newly appointed officers bought a nice new uniform, very fancy, very expensive, best of gold braid, none better. At work it soon became apparent that more than one uniform was essential; in very fact, one with less expensive braid, amongst other things! White shirts and collars, the latter detached and requiring starching, were also a problem, but not too bad when one was living ashore. Nonetheless, the collar bit was usually resolved by the purchase of a couple of celluloid collars which could be home-washed each night very easily!

There remained the problem of clothes on watch. Jim Palmer solved it by buying an army battledress and having it dyed. From then on, watchkeeping attire in the engine room was just that, with a blue shirt and sometimes overalls (called 'boiler suits'), none of which was much welcomed in the wardroom except for transient appearances on some kind of short-term business.

One more item of clothing appeared early in the kit of some of the officers; that was an anti-flash hood, a cotton balaclava-type of hood intended to minimize burns from cordite fires. Cordite fires were totally unlikely in the engine room, but I wore it anyway in action on the surface, along with safety glasses!

David Dauphinee, ERA2

Dauphinee as Boss

One of my objectives in **Qu'Appelle** was to earn the Engine Room Watch-Keeper's Certificate, an essential qualification for being given full engineering responsibilities in a seagoing vessel. That required standing watch in the engine room and boiler rooms for six months, and learning.

Meanwhile the ship had to be run properly by those who had already earned their Certificates, and they were in charge. I was assigned to Dave Dauphinee's watch in the Engine Room, and it was under him that I had to learn. Dauphinee lost no time in letting me know what was what in the Engine Room of **HMC Qu'Appelle**. Dave was an ERA 2 (Engine Room Artificer), a Petty Officer in the RCNR, with lots of engine room experience and lots of time at sea. "Let's have something straight from the start", he said. And then proceeded to tell me that I would be 'Arch' in the Engine Room to him, and that he would call me 'Sir' outside it. Nothing could have suited me better. Dave Dauphinee became a very good friend.

The kind of thing that had to be learned, apart from the routine stuff, was exemplified one night. An engine room is normally an orderly place with a high-pitched noise of smoothly running machinery. That night, pandemonium broke out, as steam and water started spouting out of strange places, scalding water escaped from the throttles, the generator stopped, and most of the lights went out. After they had happened one learned how to cope with such things, but before they happened they were a coarse threat all the time. The emergency that night had a simple cause; someone in one of the boiler rooms had paid insufficient attention, too much water went into the boiler, and water had gone over the top with the steam. Dave, and others who had the Watch-Keeper's Certificate, were presumed to know how to deal with any emergency, including one of that kind, and most did.

It was important too to learn about the operation of the boiler rooms, and I enjoyed standing watch there for a time with StoPO George Stone. But the engine room was a far more interesting and exciting place, with much more to see and learn about there, so there I spent most of my time, with David Dauphinee, ERA2.

Dauphinee and the Stokers

Dauphinee, twenty-eight years old, was from the West Coast, from Vancouver. In this he was like many of his fellows in the Naval Reserve. The Royal Canadian Naval Reserve started its existence as the 'Fishermen's Reserve' in British Columbia in the 1920s; by 1939, there were less than 300 of all ranks in it. Fishermen and Merchant seamen on both our coasts had their own peculiar qualities, qualities that led the Official Historian of the Royal Canadian Navy (Joseph Schull) to write of them: "... men, whose knowledge of coastal waters was valuable, but whose determined independence of outlook made them difficult naval material." So grudging was his appreciation of the Naval Reserve, the NR, that they don't even figure in the Index to the official history. My friend Dave Dauphinee maybe made difficult naval material, but

Some of the "stoker crew", l to r back: Sto1 George Soames from Windsor, ERA Dauphinee, AStoPO Wm. Richards from Santago Sask., LSto William Ayer from Moncton; front: A/Sto1 Wesley Doering from Sylvania Sask., Sto1 Gordon Walsh from St. Catherines ex Sto M. Harper

he was a great asset to any ship he served in. He was old enough to have been in the bootleg trade, and probably was, as many of his friends and acquaintances were. Indeed most of the older men in the Royal Canadian Naval Reserve, with ranks of Petty Officers and Warrant Officers, and some few with much higher rank, had done their time as bootleggers. It was, perhaps, the bootlegging background that led to the "snooty" attitude of the Official Historian. But for all his attitude, the men of the NR knew the sea and ships, and Dauphinee knew well the things that made ships go.

He was extraordinarily patient in his explanations and teaching in the engine room through those months of 1944. For the stokers who worked under him in the engine room he was a hard taskmaster, and brooked no idleness. He left no doubt in their minds who was boss. But, for all his tough, old-salt exterior, he had a soft and affectionate heart. On watch one night, a mug of Kye in hand, he stood surveying the stokers working at polishing the brass. Stokers, you should know, were not regarded with the greatest of kindness by their compatriots in the Naval Service. In years long gone they were the ones who shovelled coal, and were called "The Black Gang". With the coming of oil they no longer shovelled coal, but still did the hard and dirty work of the boiler and engine rooms. Pensively, Dave watched them at work and turned to me. "You know," he said, "I'm not in love with these fellows, or anything, mind. But it would break my heart to see any of them get hurt." He ordered them about mercilessly, swore at them, stood over them sternly, charged them if need be, but in very fact he did love them. They in turn were devoted to him, and would do anything for him; Dave Dauphinee was a great leader and manager of men, and an education for all who knew him.

Davey's Pants

The English Channel in the first few weeks after D-Day was a hectic place, with many U-boats appearing unexpectedly and close to the Allied ships cruising there to prevent their passage. Crews were tired out from being called frequently to action stations at all hours. This, then, presented the stage for a little drama of pathos and human nature. Dauphinee was one of those tired out, and off watch lay in his bed sleeping the sleep of the just and the true. As he lay sleeping in the crowded ERA's Mess a U-boat appeared close to the ship leading to a frantic effort to catch it with depth charges. The Mess cleared in a flash—except for Davey, in a great fright, his "nerves all shot", and unable in the darkness to find his trousers (as he later reported in the engine room).

Somehow he had missed learning about the Captain's intentions. Off watch, he had turned in to his hammock in the PO's Mess, and the lights were out. Against all habit and rules he had removed some parts of his clothing to sleep more soundly. Being below decks when there is a loud noise in the surrounding waters is not a particularly pleasant experience in time of war. Davey had already been torpedoed once, so he knew what such noises indicated.

This time he was aroused rudely as the ship was struck by a thunderclap, by a direful din. In the dark, and in panic, he tumbled out of his hammock, and immediately sought his pants. They were not to be found with any amount of groping. In despair at being unable to find them, David Dauphinee, my very good friend, then sat himself down on a bench, said to himself, "Well, Davey, I guess this is it", and waited. Waited—for the end.

He told the story on himself when he later came on watch. Everyone laughed heartily, including Dave himself. But I couldn't help thinking of him sitting there in the dark, alone, resigned, waiting.

The Wardroom

The wardroom was the gathering place for all officers, other than the Captain, in port, and for meals at all times. The Captain was not a wardroom officer, and could enter it only if invited. In port, one of the pleasures was having the bar open, and some of the residents made liberal use of it. The Captain's standing orders that monthly bar bills of over £5 were not allowed was got around at times by having others, less given to big bills, sign the chits for a while. Even so, there was seldom any drunkenness in the wardroom. At sea there was no drinking at all, and the bar was closed. I saw this rule breached only once, by bridge officers, after a nasty night of action.

Mealtime, and other times in the wardroom, were times of great banter, laughing, small talk, and relaxation. Almost all of the talk was very small, and on common barroom topics. Chief sat in his deep armchair in the corner saying little and with obvious disapproval on his face at times. We were fortunate that no deep antagonisms appeared in the wardroom, however. One of our unpleasant duties in the wardroom was censoring the outgoing mail. The Doctor had censoring as one of his responsibilities, but everyone pitched in to help in busy times—if we hadn't, the mail would have had to go out uncensored, it was so voluminous. Usually censoring was a very cursory thing, and letters were skipped through very quickly. It was, nonetheless, unpleasant to read, and to see others reading, mail that was not theirs.

The other side of the mail business was about that coming in to the ship. Usually it came in a great pile when the ship arrived in port, came and assuaged a terrible longing on the part of every one of the crew, a longing that ate and ate at a man's heart. But it did come and it was distributed, some of it as thin envelopes, and some as packages. The former had priority and caused the ship to go silent for a while as they were read once and twice again. The packages contained all kinds of good things, usually to eat or to wear; if they were to eat, most of the recipients would share their goodies with their messmates, though some would hoard them privately. The arrival of mail was a great occasion, magically restorative of morale and spirit to such an extent that the senders could hardly have imagined.

The Wardroom in **HMCS** **Qu'Appelle**, *showing the dining table in the foreground, the sitting room to the left, with Dr. Frost, Chief Palmer, and No. 1 McCully. The picture was obviously taken in port, for there are flowers in view, and the scuttles are open. Frost looks down as he times the exposure for the picture.*

Arrival in port also brought official dispatches and communications, some of which became part of intense and fearful wardroom discussion. Amongst the buzzes and rumours circulating in the ship while based in Plymouth the worst had to do with the dreaded E-boat. A very fast motor-torpedo boat, it was rumoured to be present in large numbers in the Channel, and would be our nemesis. In the event, we saw nary a one. They were more of a problem further east, from Dover around the Kentish coast, but none appeared in the wider waters of the western Channel. Another real worry was the snorkel U-boat, a boat which could charge its batteries with only a small tube breaking the surface. Air could be sucked into the boat through this device, and engine exhaust gas expelled; the tube being very small, radar had difficulty picking up the echoes from it, making the submarine much less vulnerable. Apparently, running with the diesels through the snorkel was very unpleasant for the U-boat crews. A wave could cause the intake valve to close, the engines continued to run and exhaust air from the boat, and eardrums would break at times. Had we but known this it would have brought great cheer to our hearts. The information about E-boats and snorkels came to us, together with news of the progress of our armies on the continent, in the form of secret reports circulated to the ship on arrival in port and devoured by the wardroom. Such reports it should be said made the return to sea a matter of considerable anxiety and even fear, though both soon faded as seagoing routines came once again into force.

The Wardroom Steward

From ancient times, officers have had servants of one kind or another. The wardroom in a ship of war was provided with such a 'servant', a steward to look after dining and similar functions. Those functions extended to waking each officer from his slumbers by the presentation of a cup of tea. Food was prepared in the ship's galley and was usually very appetizing—chicken dinners, meat loaf, lemon pie, cake with caramel sauce. The steward collected it from the galley and laid it out in the wardroom.

Our steward was James Edwards, small, discreet, unobtrusive, competent, thorough, and always addressed by his last name. His duties in normal times centred around the officers and the wardroom. But at action stations, he had a fighting post far below the upper deck, as he helped pass the ammunition out of one of the shell-rooms. Edwards shared this essential activity with many others; not all stokers were to be found in the engineering spaces in action, as they and others laboured in the magazines and other closed spaces out of sight of the sea and of the excitement on deck. In one of those actions, LSto Doug Casselman watched horrified as a 4.7 inch shell, the cap already removed from the fuse, fell from the gun platform above him onto the rim of the shell room hatch—and from there harmlessly onto the deck at his feet. Steward Edwards was in the shell room.

Savard: The wardroom officers were, on the whole, a rather interesting bunch. One was Paul Savard, Senior Watchkeeper in the ship, Lt RCN, speaking with a Quebec accent, dark, dapper, a veteran of the

Dunkirk evacuation and of years in the Atlantic. Paul smoked cigarettes using a long slim holder and even has it in hand in the official picture of the officers. On the night *Skeena* took the ground in Reykjavik harbour, Paul came off watch at some small hour in the morning. We had that day run into Reykjavik in a gale of wind, with enormous seas, and came to anchor late in the evening, off Videy Island. Big, big winds. *Skeena*, Paul reported, had dragged anchor and gone aground. The rest of the story is in Chapter 4.

Paul, also, is memorable for his shore-going habits. Whenever the ship was in harbour and the opportunity

The officers of **HMCS Qu'Appelle**, *photographed officially one day in July of 1944, in Plymouth Harbour. Standing picture left to right – Hunter, Duff, Holmes, Campbell, Frost, Bowser, Lamont. Sitting – Clarence, MacDermid, McCully, Commander J.D. Birch, RNR, Palmer, Savard, Dadson. RCN A991*

came, Paul was ashore, dressed in his best, and off to parties or dates, or whatever. Or so he said. For me, an innocent abroad, Paul was something to behold. He had a book in preparation, he said, but seemed stuck on the first chapter. That first chapter dealt with a wardroom scene, with a pretty girl as guest, and as Paul enters an immediate spark is generated. You can see how his mind ran!

He also had the wicked sense and sensibilities of a tease. In the wardroom, when Chief Engineer Palmer was about, Paul told his best stories of the night before, told them luridly, fully, and interminably embroidered beyond any reality (which was probably of the tamest nature if told honestly), and told them for one purpose only. That was to get a rise out of Palmer who abhorred such stories. As Palmer adopted his ministerial mien, Paul would look aside to one person or another, cigarette holder at a jaunty angle reinforcing his mischief, and smile wickedly, out of Palmer's view. Savard had a sharp sense of humour anyway; writing for the ship's newsletter as "Wardroom Commentator" he wrote: "Wouldn't it be funny as hell to see Pinnochio in a beard, Gunner Harry teaching Sunday School, or Pinky McCully shooting Crap?" Each of these pictures captured an important aspect of the individual referred to.

Clarance: Then there was the Navigating Officer, Doug Clarance, Lt RCNVR, big, blond, private-schoolish. Doug suggested one day that I was an undesirable type despite the fact that we had little to do with each other. But it was he who was responsible for piloting and navigation—including the nights off the French coast amongst the rocks. For those events he had an early version of Loran aboard, and told us that he could fix our position with it within a few yards or so. He was Mentioned in Dispatches for his work on one of those nights. His assistant in the chart room, Ship's Writer PO Paul Bedard, earned the Distinguished Service Medal on the same night for calmness under fire, during the whole of the war the only such award made to a Supply Branch rating.

Doug had a peculiarity that was a trial to the bridge officers at times; it was extraordinarily difficult to rouse him from sleep. The bridge resolved the problem by instructing the messenger who roused him to stay in the chart room until he had Doug on his feet. Doug was from the west coast. After the war, he followed Chemical Engineering as a profession.

Frost: Max Frost, Surgeon Lt, RCNVR was also from the west coast. He was always full of good cheer and fun, never morose or out of sorts. Nonetheless, the broken and bleeding bodies of his shipmates on the night of Operation Dredger had a deep impact on our doctor, and one from which he never fully recovered. Max had an interest in photography, and we developed and printed pictures in his cabin from time to time (strictly illegal!). After the war, Max went back to Vancouver to practise there.

Dadson: Hank Dadson, Lt, RCNVR, turned out to be cousin to Claire, my future wife, though that really meant nothing at the time. Hank had been in **HMCS Athabaskan** when she was glider-bombed in 1943. Hank was from Manitoba, but went to Vancouver after the war and remained in the west.

McCully: Our First Lieutenant was Bill McCully, Lt, in the RCN since joining as a cadet in 1936. McCully was excitable, and probably somewhat unstable. After the war, he had a checkered career, got to be Commander, but died quite young. An acquaintance who served under him at sea for training as a cadet and who went on to a long career in the Navy thereafter, has said that he never came across anyone so able at ship handling. In the engine room, one could always tell what kind of person was issuing the orders when coming alongside; with a good ship handler, there might be as few as three orders from Slow Ahead—they would be Half Astern, Stop, Finished with Engines. A poor or uncertain ship handler, by contrast, could go through a dozen changes of speed before finishing. Ability in coming alongside is a special quality not given to all, captains or not.

One night Bill returned aboard the ship, somewhat inebriated, took the quartermaster's pistol from him, and entered the wardroom waving it. After some haggling it was taken from him by either Hunter or MacDermid, and nothing was ever said or made of the incident. But next day, at First Lieutenant's defaulters, there were ratings up before him for punishment for much less serious offences.

It was McCully who greeted me on my arrival on

the bridge the night the Captain was felled. Bill, now in command, had just arrived there himself, and when I excitedly asked for the Captain, it was he who blurted out, "What? What?" darting frenzied glances around him. Frenzied glances or not, he managed us and the ship very well until our safe return to Plymouth.

MacDermid: The 'Pinnochio' lampooned by Savard (above) in the ship's magazine was Ted MacDermid, Lt RCNVR, the Group Gunnery Officer, fresh-faced, and with a slightly upturned nose. MacDermid stayed in the Navy after the war.

Hunter: Brrrrryce Pepall (Pep) Hunter, Lt RCNVR, was full of good sense. Before joining us he was a pilot with the Fleet Air Arm. On joining the ship he had a lovely well-shaped beard, but it was gone by the time the official picture was taken. Pep was full of happy laughter and jollity. Since he had got chubby his wife had told him to come home only after losing weight, so he ate no potatoes or bread, but drank freely. That regime lost him 17 pounds in a few weeks. Hunter had served at sea with Lord Louis Mounbatten and drew our attention to the importance of leadership, telling us what a leader Mountbatten was, and that the people in his ships and fleets would follow him anywhere.

Holmes: Warrant Officer (T) Harry Holmes, RCN, was the Torpedo Officer. He was normally very stiff and straightlaced, standing very erect and properly always. Some of the wardroom officers seemed to pick on him for the fun of it, and to laugh at his reactions, but he endured such things carefully. Holmes had moved into the class of wardroom officers not long before, he was up from the lower deck through long years of service, and he was certainly a professional in his chosen field, the torpedoes, depth charges, and ammunition. This must have come from many years in the Royal Navy for Canada had no indigenous torpedo experts.

Warrant Officers in the Navy were a special class of people. They were older than other officers, by quite a bit, and were of long long experience. In Prince Rupert, Warrant Engineer Griffiths was 62 years old, possibly a record. He had been all over the world in his profession. Of most interest was what was disclosed when the Earl of Athlone visited. Seeing the ribbons, he asked Griffiths what regiment he had been in. Well! The two ribbons that led to this question were from the Boer War! His various other ribbons he didn't bother to wear. Gunner Holmes was not as old or as talkative as Warrant Engineer Griffiths, but it was clear from his manner what he thought of the brash young whippersnappers around him in the wardroom.

Murphy: Vince Murphy, Sub Lt RCN, had an unfortunate propensity, especially difficult for a man who intended the Navy to be his life's work. Vince was terribly sick at sea. He had only to hear the order to "single up lines", the prelude to slipping (leaving harbour), and he needed a bucket to go from one place to another. The bucket got carried everywhere, but never interfered with his performance as a ship's officer. Vince was a Signals Officer, but wanted above everything to get into the Fleet Air Arm, which he did a few months later. He was never happy in **Qu'Appelle**, mostly because he could not reconcile the discrepancies between his strictly disciplined and professional training in the Royal Navy with the somewhat easy organization we had. Murphy stayed in the service until retirement, and had several commands before then.

Campbell: Jack Campbell, Lt RCNVR, was anti-submarine officer, and the people who ran the ASDIC were responsible to him. Most of the time at sea, the ASDIC was in operation, unless our speed was high. At high speed, the noise of rushing water masked all other sounds, and made the ASDIC unit useless. It was a device for sending sound waves out into the water in short pulses. If there were anything within some distance of the ship, the sound would bounce off it, and an echo would be returned to the ASDIC cabinet. A good operator could interpret the echo to read from it 'submarine' or 'fish', (or 'wreck' in shallow waters), with its range and bearing. Then he would report "Echo bearing Green 35", or whatever the numbers were. The bridge of the ship was equipped with a loud speaker that repeated the ASDIC transmissions and echoes; all on the bridge were bathed in their sounds, about D above middle C as the sent pulse, a softer D below as a sort of afterthought, and D again for the echo (if there were one). As the range on a submarine closed, the time between transmission and echo decreased until, as the ship passed above the target, they merged, the increasing frequency of sounds being accompanied by a steep increase of adrenalin level in those within earshot. One of the deficiencies of the whole system was that all echo contact was lost as the ship came close to its target, and the depth charges were, in effect, dropped blind. With two stalking ships, though, one could hold the target in sight, while the other attacked.

Wade: Johnny Wade, Lt RCNVR, was Group Signals Officer. **Qu'Appelle** was Senior Officer (i.e., the lead ship) of a group of three or four, and the Group Signals Officer was responsible for signals dealing with the whole group, usually made to shore authorities. Signals had been of vital importance to fleets for hundreds of years, and Nelson's success at Trafalgar was in part attributable to his intense interest in and concern over the best possible signalling methods. Lord Mountbatten was also a signals specialist, and advanced the art of radio signalling enormously. To the crew Wade was 'Muscles' despite being rather small and dapper.

Duff: J A Duff, Paymaster Lt RCNVR, was a reserved individual, and has left little impression. But his accounting specialty made it automatic that the wardroom accounts were done up by him, so we all had a little note from him each month!

Bowser: Ed Bowser, Lt RVNCR, was an anti–submarine specialist, but his role in **Qu'Appelle** was that of staff officer to the senior officer of the group, who was our Commanding Officer.

Chief Stoker Patry

The Chief Stoker and Discipline

Chief Stoker Joseph Patry, RCN, was a professional with long experience in the Canadian Naval Service, and was the most senior Petty Officer in the ship. He was rather round of stature, round faced, dark of hair, serious, dignified, hard working, and altogether well respected. He was also the main source of information in the ship. He was always greeted with, "What's the Buzz, Chief Stoker?" and always responded, with a very serious and worried face, by reciting what was going to happen next, or sometime, or somewhere. "What's the buzz, Chief Stoker?" Chief Stoker Patry knew everything well in advance of everyone else, including the Captain. The Chief Stoker's Action Station was everywhere on deck that he might be needed, to run fire pumps, deal with fires, look after valves and pipe lines, etc. In port it was he who sounded the fuel and water tanks, and tended to their filling, so bringing him the contacts that made him so perfectly informed on everything at all times. Everyone thought himself a confidante of Chief Stoker Patry. He was a tower of strength in the Engineering Department for no one else carried the authority that he did.

Patry was responsible for discipline in the Stoker ranks. To see him march an errant rating up to the desk for Captain's or First Lieutenant's defaulters was something to behold. With a totally stern and serious face, full of disapproval, it was, "Off caps! Eyes front!" and rigid unbending deportment until the defaulter was marched away again to whatever punishment had been assigned him. With one of the defaulters one day, I had some (totally misplaced) empathy, and asked Patry if I might speak to him after the Captain had finished with his flaying. The Chief Stoker thought it might be a good idea, but his shock at the abandonment of Naval discipline was very obvious on his face when I asked him to leave me and the individual concerned alone in my cabin for our chat. In the event, the chat did no good at all, and the rigid etiquette of Naval discipline, under which Chief Stoker Patry should have been present for the whole interview, had been abandoned for nought.

On another occasion Chief Stoker Patry had need for the full power of his office. We had picked up some survivors off a tug—Americans who had been sunk off Cherbourg and had been several hours in the water. The Engineering Department washed their clothes for them, to rid them of oil and salt water, and it was found next morning that all rank insignia had been stolen from the officers' collars. The missing jewellery was obviously in the possession of some errant stokers, and Patry issued an edict. "No insignia—no leave next time in port!" In other words, "Cough up or languish." An hour later, a messenger from the Stokers' Mess arrived and turned in the missing bits; rumour had it that the Mess had been the scene of a serious row after the edict was issued.

As Others Saw the Chief Stoker

The Chief Stoker was loved by more than one of the crew, as is evident from the little biography about him that appeared in the first issue of the ship's magazine.

"It's the latest"

Here it is:

"In the PO's mess, they call him Uncle Bulgy. Actually, as he will tell you himself, he isn't really fat, he's just well protected from the cold. To you and to me, he's the Chief Stoker.

"In a way, Uncle Bulgy is a rather remarkable character. To begin with, he is of a merry disposition. He can laugh—and laugh heartily—a characteristic which you will admit is noticeably foreign to most CPOs. He has been with the service eighteen years, and those years have developed in him a keen intuition for rumours. It is well said that some day he shall doubtless disturb the residents of heaven by starting a buzz that leave is to be granted to the Nether Regions, commencing on the first.

"He is a veritable authority on all aspects of the war. Should one fail to hear the latest newscast, then Uncle Bulgy is the very man to fall back on for an up-to-date summary of events. If he gets a little ahead of Ike Eisenhower every now and again, it is only because he has convinced himself that is the way things should be. He is like that.

"It is good that he is half Irish, for if he did not have a temper beneath his cherubic smile, he'd be a most impractical fellow to have for a Chief Stoker. His men claim that when Uncle Bulgy really gets mad, several of his chins leap about at tangents to each other, and his tummy heaves about like a barrage balloon in a gale. They say it is almost terrifying.

Most of the Petty Officer staff of the Engineering Department in **HMCS** **Qu'Appelle***, as officially photographed in August 1944 in Plymouth Harbour. Naming the picture left to right, there are:* **Back row** *– Stoker POs H. Grove (Red Deer, Alb.), J. Ford (Halifax, N.S.), R. Moore (Ireland), G. Stone (Halifax, N.S.), and J. Fournier (Dartmouth, N.S.).* **Middle row** *– Engine Room Artificers J. Talbot(?) (Lenorhon, P.Q.), F. Ewald (Victoria, B.C.), E. Cook (Victoria, B.C.), D. Dauphinee (Vancouver, B.C.), J. Tate (Victoria, B.C.), C. Roy (Quebec, P.Q.), and Stoker PO A. Foley (Glace Bay, N.S.).* **Front row** *– Chief ERA R. Houston (Toronto, Ont.), Lt.Cmdr(E) Palmer (Montreal, P.Q.), Lt(E) A.G.W. Lamont (Toronto, Ont.), Chief Stoker J. Patry (Quebec, P.Q.) RCN A998*

"As Bachelors go, he is a paragon of virtue. I hope St Peter takes stock of the fact that Uncle Bulgy is invariably absent when fishy reminiscences are being aired in the mess. People have said that 'He's above looking at things in that light'. However, with an eye to his ample proportions, I would assume it difficult for him to see it by any light.

"I give you Chief Stoker Patrick Patry as a good fellow!" And so he was.

The Engine Room Department Goes to Sea

The whole of the crew in a ship like **Qu'Appelle** was organized into departments, watches, action stations, duties, etc. The Engine Room Department, in turn, was organized as shown in the Watch List, one of the lists posted periodically to advise all of their duties in the coming days. "Steaming watches", in general, applied when the ship was not in harbour; in harbour other lists of duties were in force and, at that time, groups were off on shore leave.

Steaming watches began before leaving harbour for the boilers had to be got going. If they were cold, this meant slowly getting up a head of steam, and with it getting the various steam-driven pumps and fans into service.

But the really careful part had to be the engines. Steam turbine engines are made of metallic parts, and metallic parts get larger when they are heated. The steam used to drive them is very hot at 700° F for, after all, the engines are *heat* engines. That hot steam heats up everything it touches. With the watch–like nature of a steam turbine, parts cannot be allowed to grow helter-skelter as they heat up, or they will touch and run into each other when they start to move.

These aspects of the engines were dealt with by heating them slowly. A special engine or motor, called the turning gear, turned the main engines slowly, as

STEAMING WATCHES ENGINE ROOM DEPARTMENT – STEAMING 24/1/4..

RED WATCH

ROY C.	E.R.A.	ENG.ROOM.
TALBOT	E.R.A.	"
CASSELMAN	L/STO.	"
CALLAGHAN	STO.	"
McKENZIE	STO.	"
FORD	S.P.O.	BLR.ROOM.
FREEMAN	S.P.O.	"
ROSS	STO.	"
HILL	STO.	"
McANDREW	STO.	"
HARPER	STO.	

WHITE WATCH

DAUPHINE	E.R.A.	ENG.ROOM.
EWALD	E.R.A.	"
AYER	L/STO.	"
DOERING	STO.	"
WALSH	STO.	
MOORE	S.P.O.	BLR.ROOM.
GROVE	S.P.O.	"
SINCLAIR R.	STO.	"
BROEN	STO.	"
VINETTE	STO.	"
CROWELL	STO.	

BLUE WATCH

TATE	E.R.A.	ENG.ROOM.
COOK.	E.R.A.	"
TELFORD	L/STO.	"
SINCLAIR R.	STO.	"
HONOUR	STO.	
STORE	S.P.O.	BLR.ROOM.
FOLEY	S.P.O.	"
TRUDEL	STO.	"
CURRIE	STO.	"
GRAHAM	STO.	"
McPHERSON	STO.	

STAND BY THIRD BOILER

FOURNIER	S.P.O.
FICHARDS	A/S.P.O.
GALLOP	SPO.
ARISS	STO.
TAYLOR.	STO.
WAUGH	STO.
GRAFF	STO.

DIESEL DYNAMO – ACTION STATIONS.

SOANES	STO.
MORGAN	STO.

WILL REMAIN ON UNTILL ACTION STATIONS ARE OVER.

DAY WORK

MURRAY	E.R.A.	AS REQUIRED.
STINGMAR	E.R.A.	AS REQUIRED.
FOURNIER	S.P.O.	IN CHARGE DAY WORK.
RICHARDS	A/S.P.O.	CENTRAL STORES.
McFADDEN	L/STO.	DAY WORK.
GALLOP	STO.	"
ARISS	STO.	"
TAYLOR	STO.	"
McINNES	STO.	C.E.R.A.'s MATE.
MORGAN	STO.	WORK SHOP.
McLEAN	STO.	UPPERDECK STOKER.
MOUSSEAU	STO.	
CLEMENT	STO.	3.08s WAITER.
SOANES	STO.	CENTRAL STORES.
CRABB P.	STO.	E.R.A's MESS.
WALKER	STO.	S.P.O's MESS.
WAUGH	SPO.	STOKERS' MESS.
TAYLOR	STO. →	

CHANGES HAVE NOW STARTED TO TAKE PLACE BETWEEN ENGINE ROOM AND BOILER ROOM RATINGS.IT IS UP TO THESE RATINGS TO PICK UP THEIR DUTIES AS SOON AS THEY CAN AND GIVE OTHERS A CHANCE TO CHANGE AROUND.

A.Palmer
LIEUT.CMDR. (E).

Q.Fermont
LIEUT. (E).

CH/STOKER.

steam was allowed into them at a low rate. In this way, the whole circumference of the rotor of the engine and of the related fixed blades was uniformly heated, and so didn't distort out of shape and touch parts it would be damaged by. Warming the engines through in this way took some hours. The boilers, too, had to be started up slowly, to avoid distortion and damage. Elsewhere here, a little table giving our days at sea and in harbour refers to the time in harbour as 'Four hours' notice' or 'One hour's notice' or 'Immediate notice'; these time references indicated how far the Engine Room Department could allow the machinery to be from heated through and Ready In All Respects For Sea. On Immediate Notice the engines remained turning slowly and well heated through at all times, and a full steaming watch was maintained.

The time to leave came inevitably, and the Bosun passed through the ship, piping on his whistle, and calling, "Hands to stations for leaving harbour! Special sea-duty men close up!" Loud speakers were for unusual things, not for the time-honoured orders that sent men to their duties. Then from the bridge, the cry, "Single up lines! Cast off for'd. Cast off aft. Take in the spring!" and we were away. In the engine room, the orders came by telegraph, calling for Slow Ahead, or Slow Astern, or Stop, or whatever, depending on the situation of the ship in relation to others, to wind, to tide, and to the skipper's abilities and peccadilloes.

And slowly the ship traversed the calm waters of the harbour, approaching a magic moment. At some point, whether one were in the engine room or on deck, a movement beneath one's feet began, began and continued, as the ship responded to the movement of the sea, the slow swell portending more to come. Once away from harbour, all shore-going routines were abandoned, and sea watches and routines ruled. But for a true seaman the separation from land had taken place at the magic moment of the first sensation of movement beneath his feet.

Larne and Workups and The Ship's Competence

For a week or two before D–Day we had 'workups'. This is a period of training in various aspects of operating the ship—anti-submarine operations, anti-aircraft fire, etc, etc. There was a very senior Royal Navy officer in charge of workups at Larne, just north of Belfast Loch in Ireland, seen by all as a feared taskmaster indeed. We did all the usual things in the way of finding and holding onto a submarine, trying to hit a drone aircraft towed by another, firing off the guns, dropping depth charges, responding to cries of "fire", etc. Marks (as in school!) were assigned by the officers in charge of the Larne operations; in general, our marks were not very good. I hang my head to say it, but one night I actually missed the whole business while sleeping before going on watch. The noise of everything going on was deafening, but I heard none of it. No one noticed my absence!

In retrospect it is of great interest that the crew in

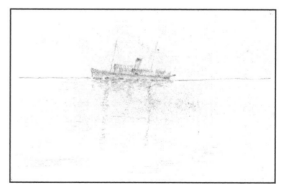

The Admiral's ship, **HMS Philante**, *at the Larne training area.*

Qu'Appelle, and no doubt in almost all other Canadian ships, was an amateur crew on the whole, even including many of the permanent people. In general they didn't have a whole-hearted fear and worry about their own inadequacies or incompetencies, and probably did not even recognize that any such things existed. Indeed, it seemed as if life was rather routine, and problems in action would be dealt with in whatever way made sense at the time. According to Pep Hunter, this was not the case in the vessels or groups that Lord Louis Mountbatten had charge of. But there were others besides him who were profoundly professional in their approach to their duties, one being the famous Captain Walker, RN, who developed and applied the idea of hunter-killer groups for dealing with submarines. Another was Cmdr "Chummy" Prentice, a professional of professionals in the Canadian Naval Service, and *Qu'Appelle's* Commanding Officer in the last months of 1944. The author, indeed, was a prime example of the amateurishness of some of those at sea in HMC ships or, at least, in HMCS *Qu'Appelle*!

It also needs saying that money and funding had an enormous effect on our competence. *Qu'Appelle* burned 13 tons of oil an hour at Full Speed (a battleship would burn 75 tons an hour). One trip on our part would consume as much oil as the whole Canadian Navy was allowed annually before the war. Restrictions on consumption applied not only in the peacetime Navy. The amount of powder and shot of various kinds that could be used in practice firing of guns, torpedoes, and other armament was very little. In effect, people had to learn to be good at these things through use in action. Probably the expenditure in times of practice should have amounted to twice that in real situations, if high competence and professionalism were to be assured.

Amongst the things that have survived the years and are now in the National Archives are copies of *Qu'Appelle's* "Return on Ammunition Expended" for the summer months of 1944. The numbers are here at the top of the next page.

These returns were made to the shore authorities, and were part of the required paperwork in the Royal Navy. The officer responsible for making the return was Gunner Holmes. With his Royal Navy background it must have grieved him that the Canadian shore authorities told us one day that the forms were "no longer required". Fortunately for this story, he continued for a month or two longer anyway! Habit, long-ingrained, is hard to change, especially a habit of such a professional (and bureaucratic) nature.

Invasion Months

Out of Plymouth, HMCS *Qu'Appelle* was senior ship, or leader, of a group of four Canadian destroyers, all River Class, and most originally British ships. In our group, EG12 and later EG11, were *Skeena*, *Saskatchewan*, and *Restigouche*. We always operated as a group, starting just before D-Day (though maybe we also did so out of Londonderry in April–May?) On June 4 we sailed from Plymouth, passing the many ships in the harbour crowded with troops. At a meeting in the wardroom, the Captain had informed us that D–Day had arrived, and we were to be in the Channel entrance,

ITEM	NUMBER USED	
	June	July-Sept
For 4.7 in. guns		
Cartridges	7	244
Shell	7	271
Fuses	7	284
For 20 mm. guns		
Cartridges	1959	3853
Rockets		
Flares 2 in	0	94
Snowflake	0	8
Hedgehog		
1 3/4 in	72	264
Practice	0	48
Depth Charges	21	0

to stop the hordes of submarines sure to come (many came, but no hordes). So that was why we were at sea on the 4th, ready for D-Day on the 5th. Despite the great train of ships passing, intended for the Mulberry Harbour installations, the weather forced a postponement, and the affair didn't start until the 6th.

We saw little of the actual D–Day events, other than passing aircraft and ships, but had our own interests over the next days and months. Some of it is recited in other stories here, but there were small things too. Like picking up that half a dozen Americans from a Carley raft one day off the Channel Islands. Ferrying a small tug to Cherbourg, they had got off course, drawn enemy fire from shore, and were sunk. They got off course, perhaps, because their only chart was a map taken from a page of *Time* magazine, they said. They were glad to

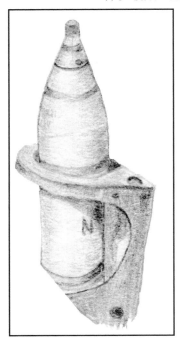

A "ready-use" shell at the X-gun mount.

see us, of course, rather than the German ships which were also floating about here and there. Having arrived aboard, the senior of them asked to be taken to our Captain, to whom he said, "Sir, you are in dangerous waters!" News from any quarter, one would suppose, is welcome. It was they who accounted for the Chief Stoker's edict already referred to.

In those days, the ship was full of rumours and worries. "What's the buzz, Chief Stoker?" we asked, and like as not got the reply that we would be glider bombed that day, the bomber being homed in by the German aircraft that had been shadowing the group. And so we were. Glider bombs were winged bombs, guided through radio control by the pilot of the mother aircraft. They were not terribly accurate, though terribly worrisome to the bridge officers! Nicknamed "Chase Me Charlies", they followed a ship, but it was relatively easy to turn and outrun their area of manoeuvrability. Athabaskan, in 1943, had been struck by one of them. However this time the bomb fell harmlessly astern (thanks to our gunners, according to the Captain's report), giving us only a bad jolt, and a big noise in the engine room.

On the days after D–Day the threatened U-boats seemed to have appeared exactly as the Chief Stoker had told us to expect. Our Group had, at any rate, seemed to detect one on the evening of the 7th June. Detection, identification, and holding onto the detected sound were very difficult in the Channel, for it was shallow, full of tidal currents, with fish and wrecks all over the place; all of these things confused the echo patterns of ASDIC and gave the ASDIC operator a very difficult task. But it soon became very evident that some of what seemed to be echoes from a U-boat were very real. With four destroyers poking around after him for over a full day, this particular U-boat captain had nerve and courage to spare, launching many torpedoes at the group, though ineffectively. The U-boat crews were in the service of the Devil himself, but in that service they gave evidence of the highest courage. This time they had one of the tools that we had been dreading for so long, the Acoustic torpedo, known in the ships as Gnats.

The Gnat had put numerous ships on the bottom. Fitted with noise detectors, this infernal device homed in on the sound of a ship's propellers and machinery. When its use seemed like a possibility because a submarine was thought to be in the neighbourhood, speeds were reduced to 5-6 knots, and the Cat was streamed. The Cat was the simplest of devices invented by some Canadian genius in one of HMC Ships. He simply took two steel bars, about half an inch in diameter and 3 feet long, mounted in parallel a half inch apart, and attached to a bridle so that, when towed astern, the bars lay athwart the course. Towed thus the two bars vibrated back and forth and clashed each against the other making a dreadful racket. A different and far more complicated device, FOXER, had been invented earlier in the laboratories of Britain, set up to deal specifically with new German weapons. In fantasy we can imagine the guys in the Genius sections of Admiralty, the Bods, the day the news of the Acoustic Torpedo broke. They had just come in for the day after a breakfast of kippers and dried eggs. Probably belching a bit. "Well, lads," says the Commander, "the Acoustic Torpedo is real. What'll we do about it?" "Well, sir," says one of them, "we could take these lengths of chain …" and went on to describe his gadget. I suppose it was used by ships at sea, but not those of **Qu'Appelle's** groups—it was complicated, cumbersome to stream or pick up, expensive, slow to be provided, and regarded unhappily at sea. The Canadian CAT was simple. From whichever apparatus, however, the racket was far too much for ASDIC to manage, so that the gear couldn't be towed at all times.

And so it happened that periodically, in the many ships in the war against the U-boat, the order would pass, "Stream the Cat!" It was not a happy order to hear, but the device itself was a great comfort, for it worked. We had the Cat streamed intermittently many times in those days—whenever it seemed to the Captain or the First Lieutenant to be the prudent thing to do.

The problem arising from interference with ASDIC in the Channel was serious. ASDIC represented the eyes of a ship on the surface, eyes with which it could detect a submarine below. It did this by projecting short pulses of sound into the water, and listening for their return. Those return pulses could be deciphered by the expert operator, to tell whether they were fish, or currents, or a steel hull and, if the latter, how far away it lay and in what direction. All of this was a subtle process, one so delicate that it was unable to survive the infernal racket of a CAT gear a few hundred feet away. Again, Canadians rose to the challenge; Lt(E) John Dyke, RCNVR, one of the mechanical engineers from the University of Toronto, devised methods for silencing the CAT temporarily and at will, without retrieving it from the depths. Interestingly, recognition for doing so came to him only forty years later, and then only in the form of a newspaper story on the development. The development itself was a great help to some ships, though not to **Qu'Appelle** and others in their activities in the English Channel as it came too late.

The prolonged search immediately after D-Day, it is now known, was not for one U-boat, but several. On the evening of the 7th, a torpedo exploded alongside **Saskatchewan**, soaking her decks, and another two hundred feet astern of **Qu'Appelle**. They came from U984, commanded by Heinz Sieder, who claimed to have sunk one of us. He didn't. Later he damaged a frigate (**HMS Goodson**), and four freighters of the invasion fleet. In August he and all his crew were killed in the Bay of Biscay by **HMCS Chaudiere** and **HMCS Kootenay.** At midnight on the 7th, U621 (Hermann Stuckmann) tried again, firing at EG12, but heard only end-of-run detonation; various other of his attacks on vessels of the invasion fleet over the next two weeks were also unsuccessful, except for a minor LST being sunk. In mid-August he too was destroyed in Biscay with all his crew, by the same two Canadian destroyers along with **HMCS Ottawa**. On the morning of the 8th, U953 (Karl-Heinz Marback) had a try, firing four torpedoes at the ships of EG12, three of which exploded close but harmlessly; in the following month, it managed to sink one freighter before returning to base with an exhausted crew. This boat survived the war, eventually surrendering at Trondheim, Norway. While water conditions in the Channel helped shield the U-boats from ASDIC, it had also the (for them) unfortunate effect of interfering with the run of torpedoes, so saving us and others of their targets.

DATE SUNK 1944	U-BOAT	CREW KILLED
8 June	441	All 51
10 June	821	50
12 June	1191	All 50
18 June	767	48
24 June	971	1
25 June	269	12
29 June	988	All 50
18 July	672	0
26 July	214	All 48

The Kriegsmarine deployed forty-three U-boats into the Channel in the month of June. Some of the evidence for their presence is to be found in the record of the destruction they experienced. The table shows that destruction (primarily from air attack) in June and July in the area approximately enclosed by N/S lines through Cherbourg and just west of Brest, the area in which **Qu'Appelle** was operating. The record is rather astonishing; obviously Dönitz was shaken by his losses and the lack of successes for there were no more until December!

Amongst our buzzes and rumours the worst and most feared had to do with the dreaded E-boat. A very fast motor torpedo boat, it was rumoured to be present in large numbers in the Channel, and would be our nemesis. In the event, we saw nary a one. They were more of a problem further east, from Dover around the Kentish coast, but none appeared in the wider waters of the western Channel. Another real worry was the snorkel U-boat. Information about E-boats and snorkels came to us, with other news, in the form of secret reports circulated to the ship on our arrival each time in port, devoured by the wardroom, and made subject to endless debate.

While in port (Devonport) we went ashore into Plymouth—bombed and ruined—to the Cathedral, to the business area, to the residential areas, and to the Hoe. It was pleasant to see the normal life about despite the ruins.

The Tribal Class Destroyers

Operating out of Plymouth at the time were various Tribal Class destroyers, some of them Canadian. The ships of the Tribal Class were relatively new (1942 and 1943), heavy and powerful; they carried six 4.7 inch guns in three turrets, and an additional two 4 inch anti-aircraft weapons. Canada had four such ships, **Athabaskan**, **Haida**, **Huron**, and **Iroquois**; the first was lost in the Channel in late April of 1944, and Iroquois was engaged in runs to Gibraltar. The other two, **Haida** and **Huron**, were active near us in the Channel. We heard of them constantly, along with **Tartar** and **Ashanti** of the RN, and **Blyskawica** of the Polish Navy, with whom they operated. (**Blyskawica** in her career took part in the destruction of the astounding total of 16 U-boats! Neither **Tartar** nor **Ashanti** accounted for a single one; their victories were in actions against surface vessels.)

As **Qu'Appelle's** group stood at action stations one dark night, a similar but larger group lay some miles off, intruders into the Channel, powerful, deadly to us. It was a group of Narvik and Elbing Class German destroyers out of Brest and bent on damaging the flow of vessels to the invasion beaches of France. On board **Qu'Appelle** no one was feeling very happy at the thought of this force so close, a force clearly much stronger than our own, carrying larger guns and many more of them, faster, more numerous, thoroughly hostile, and bent on no good for us. The Captain thought to speak to the ship that night. It was not uncommon for him to do so, as he moulded the pride and morale of the crew, raising it from its earlier spiritless pit. "This is the Captain," said he over the ship's address system. "This is the Captain up here on the bridge. As you all know by now, there's a force of German destroyers lying not far away, and moving closer. That's why we are at action stations. They are big strong ships, each carrying several 5 inch guns to our two 4 inch. There's a group of our Tribals moving up too. Now, I know you are brave men, and I'm brave too. But this is no place for us, and we are getting the hell out. Wish the Tribals good shooting. We'll secure from action stations as soon as we are well clear." In the event, the Tribals came to action, one of their very successful ones, doing a good deal of damage to the German vessels. (This action is described in detail in *The Far Distant Ships*.)

Any Weapon to Hand

Most people know that the greatest drudgery a sailor faced was the cleaning of potatoes, and that they loved doing it. One fine day not long after D-Day, LSto Douglas Casselman and Sto Stanley Callaghan were exercising their skills on a bucketful of potatoes, talking and yarning about abstruse and delicate subjects connected with their recent visit to Plymouth. Blissfully happy, they were startled by the sudden appearance of a periscope a stone's throw off the side of the ship. Having no stones, they immediately, and without waiting for orders, began pelting the submarine with potatoes. Seeing the volleys directed at his ship, the U-boat captain immediately withdrew.

Meanwhile, Commander McKillop on the bridge, engaged in a prolonged search for a persistent and aggressive submarine while his ship moved ahead slowly, had also seen the volleys launched by eager members of his own crew. Deciding he could do better, he brought the ship around and had depth charges fired. Unfortunately, they did no better than the potatoes. The ship's speed being rather slow, they did succeed in giving those of us in the engine room a very big jolt, and a bigger scare. The potatoes had not even been noticed there. Nor were they accepted by the ship's A/S authorities as suitable for routine use as weapons. All things considered, however, Casselman and Callaghan were well pleased with their own performance.

The Battle of the Black Stones

Operation Dredger, one of Canada's few true destroyer actions, came about on the night of 5/6 July. British Intelligence had heard from French spies that two submarines, escorted by three anti-aircraft ships, would be leaving Brest and proceeding to sea.

By July of 1944 the U-boat arm of the Kriegsmarine could almost be said to be beleaguered, had failed in its primary aim of interrupting the flow of goods to

Britain, was totally ineffective against the Overlord invasion, and its boats were now at serious risk even close to "home" in the French ports. U-boats in the Bay of Biscay had come to expect attack by aircraft fitted with powerful search lights, and to deal with such an attack were escorted when leaving Brest by a strong force of surface vessels provided with anti-aircraft guns. Dredger was intended to provide them with a total surprise by sea in the very precincts of Brest itself.

Interception by EG12 (**Qu'Appelle**, **Saskatchewan**, **Skeena**, and **Restigouche**) was to be near Ushant, the operation being close to shore and the rocks. The story of the resulting Battle of the Black Rocks has been told in numerous books, especially in Alan Easton's *Fifty North*. Doug Clarance, as Pilot, had the trying task of keeping track of the ship's position in the dark, with rocks close by, and various ships milling around at high speed, and many changes of speed and course. How a Navigator manages in such circumstances is almost beyond understanding, as it is difficult enough even in a sailboat moving at a sedate 5 knots.

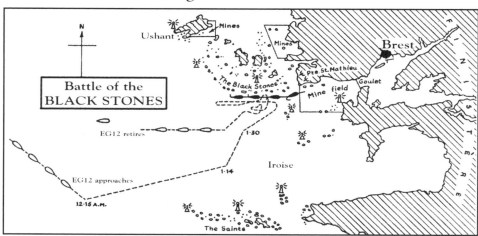

But Clarance had some help, in the way of Loran. That is a system of radio waves put out by shore stations. Every spot on the sea is a point at which the two sets of waves cross, and each point has a different signal to be read out on the Loran receiver. The system was new at the time, but became very common after the war. Without it, manoeuvring close to rocks at night would have been impossible; Loran gave our position within a few dozen feet.

Hank Dadson, one of the officers on the bridge that night, has written the following description of the action as seen from the bridge:

"Our approach by four RCN destroyers was from the south, and as the enemy proceeded to sea our line fell in astern following out from the port of Brest. As we closed the contacts, the enemy, discovering our ships, fired recognition signals. We replied with a rocket spread to illuminate them, and went to Full Power to sweep up past their line. Unknown to us, *Saskatchewan*, second ship in line and with a foul bottom, didn't get her revs on fast enough, and fell to over a quarter mile astern (close order is 200 yards separation), thus holding up the third and fourth ships as well; so *Qu'Appelle* was proceeding virtually alone. At the same time, from astern we could engage only one 2 lb gun (under control by Pep Hunter) and the forward 4.7 in gun, but at full power our own spray from the bow virtually put our guns under water. So nothing was happening, and we soon lost our element of surprise.

"I can remember the Captain shouting at Guns— 'Guns, your gunnery is bloody awful.' In the meantime we were drawing the fire from five enemy ships which thankfully seemed in large part to be going over well above us. It was later felt that the enemy had overestimated our distance from them, and were firing perhaps for 2,000 yards when in fact we were 1,000 yards abreast. When we had completed our run up we altered 180º to again run down the line. The overall picture was much improved from our standpoint. All our ships fired all their torpedoes but there were no hits as far as we know. Although the action took place inside the range of the enemy coastal guns no fire from ashore was observed, perhaps because of the melee of friend and foe.

"As *Qu'Appelle* passed back down the line, the Flak ships seemed out of it and the two submarines had turned about and were making back towards Brest. *Qu'Appelle* gave chase, but as we passed in front of one of the sinking Flak ships, we started taking some direct hits from the enemy who apparently still had a forward gun in action. The Captain ordered an alteration to starboard, and we were immediately hit within the bridge. The explosion was near the Captain, who was badly wounded; Jeanotte, the telegraphist, standing next to the Captain, and Beauchamp, Oerlikon gunner, were both mortally wounded. Shrapnel was spread throughout the bridge personnel, but because of our Canadian life-jackets, well padded with kapok fill, the shrapnel penetrated only the lower parts of the bodies (buttocks and legs). I was at the forward part of the bridge as Illumination Officer, and farthest from the explosion, and being protected by the others was the only one left standing. Savard, the Action Officer of the Watch, was down, and fell again in trying to get up. I called to him that I had control, brought the ship to midships, and disengaged on course 180°. The First Lieutenant was summoned (in action the First Lieutenant was stationed in a different part of the ship to reduce risk), and he took control. The duty of Senior Officer was passed to one of the other ships, and the action was broken off. The Yeoman, Bloomfield, although wounded, put out a fire on the bridge, and was awarded the DSM."

And so Dadson ends his story:

"It was estimated that we took 122 hits, 22 of them 'major'. As trivia, we each made an estimate of lapsed time for the operation. The estimates ran from ten minutes to over an hour. The actual time was 55 minutes. I often wonder what would have happened if the Captain had followed the submarines right into Brest Harbour!"

Well, fortunately, he didn't. For all the people on the bridge, having seen the imminence of death from the stream of fire above their heads, it was no doubt a great relief. In the engine room our own guns had been recognizable from the depth and rumble of their noise, and incoming fire from its sharp crack. There, we were not exposed to the sight of tracer fire streaming directly at us, the scythe of death just above our heads, and had the protection of the quarter inch of steel in the ship's sides. Besides, we were very low in the ship, as compared with those on the bridge. The decks, after the action, were littered with shell fragments, and the funnels made into colanders, full of holes. It was the noise that led to our first experience with a panic—

stricken person. One of the engine room crew, eyes full of fear at each crack, crept towards the starboard access ladder, and there crouched lower and lower until he was soon on the deck in fetal position.

In the days of wooden ships, when a captain saw that he would be taking a broadside in his own bows or stern, he would often give the order for the crews below to lie down. In this position there was less chance of their being struck as balls and splinters whizzed through the wide open spaces of the gun decks. We were not subject to a raking broadside, nor in that kind of ship, and no order to lie down was ever passed in a ship of iron and steel, as there was no advantage in it. Dauphinee showed his stature as a man that night for he told us to pay no attention to our prostrate comrade, and afterwards said nothing to anyone of the panic that had been displayed.

To report a problem with the steering, Palmer ordered me out of the engine room to take a message to the bridge. On deck there was a fearsome sight, beautiful in a dreadful way. There would be a flash, then a red ball going off into the distance in a flat parabola. A hit would be marked by a great red eruption and showers of sparks. Then off would go a great number of red balls almost simultaneously from a gun of smaller calibre, also producing sparks from hits. All the time, the parabolas changed shape, as the ships moved about, firing now at right angles to us, and now parallel.

Along the deck on the side away from the incoming fire, the torpedo crews were huddled in the lee of the now-empty torpedo tubes, making themselves very small. Moving fast, I found the ladder running up the outside of the bridge structure, climbed it, arrived on the bridge, and looked around stupidly, asking for the Captain. He lay on the deck, and the First Lieutenant took my message in a state of great excitement.

Despite the Captain's expressed frustration with his Gunnery Officer, at least one of the German vessels was apparently destroyed. A German High Command Communique was issued on July 8 saying:

> "The night before last, in the area of Brest, an engagement was fought between four German patrol boats and four enemy destroyers. Two destroyers were set on fire. One of our own boats was lost after an heroic fight. Part of her crew was saved."

The carnage we had wreaked in the German vessels got never a thought from us. In fact, not long after the events that morning, McCully turned up in the wardroom, and, ordering a drink (never done at sea!) from Edwards, proceeded to spout hatred and anger at the other side for having so severely injured a number of the crew of **Qu'Appelle**, ignoring the far more damaging effect we had clearly had on the enemy.

The surprise so close to home was such a shock to the Kriegsmarine that for the remainder of July it established a new defensive patrol of U-boats off Brest. A total of ten boats, in successive pairs, were occupied on such patrols. They accomplished nothing, reduced the movement of boats to the invasion area, and lost one of their number to a British mine. Their story is recorded in a footnote in C. Blair, "Hitler's U-Boat War".

Blair also identifies the two submarines ambushed by Dredger as U–741 (C.Palmgren), which escaped with damage from gunfire, and U–212 (H.Vogler). The latter, with all hands, was believed lost off Normandy a week later. The former was lost in the English Channel five weeks later with most of the crew.

As a result we had a day or so of time in Devonport while the holes were cut out and new pieces welded in. The pieces cut out and the debris of shell fragments on deck became souvenirs shared amongst the crew. For our doctor, dealing with the dreadful memories of large numbers of wounded men, souvenirs were not of interest. Until that time he had had only to deal with the kinds of complaints peculiar to seamen.

A shell hole cut out of the funnel RCN A987

On another occasion all the action had been impersonal and belonged to the theatre, as the ship's company watched awestruck and excited while the U–boat pens in Brest got bombed. We were many miles away, but the parabolic trails of vapour behind the heavy bombs could be seen easily as they lengthened, producing immense billows of smoke where they ended. For us, far off, it was like watching a movie, and easy to forget that people were dying at the ends of those trails of vapour.

Engagement in "Operation Kinetic"

By August of 1944, the German-held port of Brest was being abandoned by a traffic of vessels moving south, and the Admiralty had determined on another operation similar to Dredger, to be called "Kinetic". At Kinetic, **Qu'Appelle** was the lead ship in a group of destroyers, four Canadian (**Qu'Appelle**, **Assiniboine**, **Skeena**, and **Restigouche**) and one British (**Albrighton**), assigned to be hosts at the surprise party in Audierne Bay one night, the guests being ships from nearby German bases.

One of the new anti-submarine weapons we carried, called "Hedgehog", was a set of twenty-four bombs, propelled off spigots as a cloud from a launcher on the foredeck. Its name came from its appearance. The idea was to have one ship hold the U-boat in its ASDIC, the submarine detection system, reporting to the other the position and movements of the underwater object. The other ship would then creep along toward the proper spot to fire off the Hedgehog bombs, each carrying about thirty-five pounds of explosive. The hands manning the weapon, and the officers on the bridge, had some control over the pattern of the bombs and their direction as they left the ship. Sinking through the water, it was the hope that at least one of the bombs would strike the U-boat and explode, damaging it. The bombs were fused sensitively, and the explosion of one of them against a submarine would, in general, set off all the others, for a total of over 800 pounds of Torpex, a high explosive that brought bad news to the U-boat crews.

Going into an action on the surface, the Hedgehog

bombs, we were told, were not very desirable things to have lying around on the foredeck. There would be a heavy gun firing close to their fuses, not to speak of incoming fire setting them off. So they had to be disposed of. Possibly they could have been off-loaded and returned to the magazine, and they were in fact not terribly dangerous on the foredeck. Nonetheless, for whatever reason, they *were* off-loaded. The easy way. They were just fired off, some hours before we began our run-in to the rendezvous point. In relatively shallow water. Which meant that when they hit the bottom, they went off with a very loud roar. We all thought that the whole of the German forces in France must have heard it and divined what was going on! At 0233 in the morning, **Qu'Appelle** illuminated three enemy vessels by rocket and two minutes later opened fire, at a range of 4,700 yards. In the whole action that followed the enemy vessels were destroyed, while only one of the ships of EG12 was hit, and that only by a small shell that caused no damage.

But Operation Kinetic brought trouble, and it earned Jim Palmer the OBE (the Order of the British Empire). One of Palmer's ambitions was to be involved in some surface actions, a romantic notion arising probably from reading about Jutland. In point of fact, though **Qu'Appelle** and the other ships of her group were called "destroyers" they were not at all suited to actions of the kind classically undertaken by destroyers—surface engagements using guns and torpedoes, often against much larger vessels. They had been converted over the years to vessels strictly suited for anti-submarine action, as the armament needed for their former purposes had been reduced drastically. Except for speed, they were little better than corvettes for the kind of action Jim Palmer longed for! Operation "Kinetic" was the second surface action in which we were indeed involved (short and hot, not big and lengthy). In it, we suffered damage in the steering compartment, damage inflicted by one of our own vessels (**Skeena**), which ran into us in the midst of smoke laid by the German vessels, and into which we also had run. Palmer, who had no fixed Action Station, but responsibilities throughout the ship in action, quickly went aft see what had happened, came back to the engine room, and told us. Being stopped dead in that location was not a happy experience! However, we soon got under way, steering by varying the speed of the two engines.

Endless orders from the bridge to the engine room for adjustments in rotational speed (revs) of the two shafts were successful in keeping the ship on a wiggly course out of the scene of the action and then on for Plymouth. Our normal full speed, incidentally, was above 300 revs, with the full 35,000 HP at work. At that speed, we moved at something like 30 knots, and being on the quarterdeck was interesting, with its noise of the propellers, the big turbulence behind, the shaking and vibration, and the feeling of immense speed. The return to Plymouth was at far less than full speed! Chief Engineer Palmer was awarded the Order of the British Empire for that return and his activities in keeping the ship afloat.

The reasons we were struck by one of our own ships were complex. It happened near the rocks off

Penmarch Point on the French coast west of Lorient, in the dark, and often in smoke. That there was some confusion is hardly surprising. One of the officers on the bridge that night has described the scene there:

"Our job that night was to intercept any small craft trying to escape from Brest (which had been bombed very heavily that day). Our Captain had us in line ahead, and took us into smoke that one of the German ships had laid down. Savard, the Action Officer of the Watch, and Clarance, the Pilot, kept calling to the Captain of decreasing depths of water and distance to shore. The Captain finally signalled alteration of course by 180°. In the meantime, our second ship (**HMS *Albrighton***) followed us into the smoke, but the third ship *Skeena* took independent action and broke order. I remember having a feeling of concern or intuition and asked the Yeoman to put his glasses on starboard bow, and sure enough as we came out of the smoke there was *Skeena* bearing down on us. It was so close and steering so directly at our midships that the men on the upper deck didn't know whether to run forward or aft, but all our Captain did was to repeat twice, 'Oh, he will miss us', which to the bridge officers wasn't going to be. So Savard, on his own initiative, ordered 'Hard a port'.

"The Captain later expressed himself of the opinion that it was Savard's order that caused the collision. That was nonsense, for there was no time for port helm to alter course to port. It did, however, freeze the rudder to port, and as memory serves me, it was more than adjusting engine revs to steam ahead and steer a course. Port engine was placed ahead, and starboard engine astern."

That was the view from the bridge. But there was a reason in the Engine Room, too, for our misfortune. Our Chief Engineer believed, passionately, in fuel economy—as any good Chief Engineer should, and as described above. Believing in fuel economy, the Chief managed the engines to achieve it. Normally, we were almost never at full speed, which meant that the throttles on the engines would usually be closed in quite a bit, with a high pressure drop across the control valves. Such a pressure drop represents a loss of efficiency and a waste of fuel. An alternative is to close off some of the nozzles in the engines

*The gash in the starboard quarter of **Qu'Appelle** from collision with **Skeena** in August of 1944. The nature of the gash shows that **Skeena** struck when the two ships were at an acute angle (30° at most) to each other. **Skeena** was probably turning hard to port. Had **Qu'Appelle** been but ten feet further ahead, there would have been no collision.*

themselves, so that the full steam pressure available is used in the nozzles left open to use it. (The "nozzles" were those last parts of the steam supply system, right in the engine itself, and from which steam issued at very high velocity to enter the blades of the turbine, so causing the propeller to turn. It was those nozzles that the Chief was referring to in his letter to me, when he talked about the "running of the ship".) And so there we were, in close and hot action with some nozzles closed, and when the engine room telegraph rang for Emergency Full Ahead, we had to work away at opening them. It was a relatively slow process, and while we were doing it, we were jolted sideways off our feet—we had been struck, as we found out. No one outside the engine room ever knew about this lapse from full preparedness for action.

Two of the engine room stokers were recommended for Mention in Dispatches for their behaviour during this action.

The Stone Diary

StoPO George Stone of HMCS **Qu'Appelle**, against all rules, kept a diary. It started innocently as an account book, a small book in which he kept track of "dhobying" (clothes washing) he had done for others, and how much they owed him in consequence. But on June 3, 1944, the enormity of the events he was heading into led him to begin a record of them. That record conveys an immediacy and urgency not to be found in any long-afterwards reminiscences, though it has some inaccuracies now recognizable. Here it is:

"June 3, Irish Sea, Heading south—The Skipper's

calm voice over the SRE at Noon. 'So from now on, the ball is in the air … on your toes … that's all.' …

"June 5th; 2315 hrs, Leaving Plymouth Harbour— The Captain spoke again. Ears glued to the SRE, we listened. 'I've just returned from the operations room. The plan is this. D Hour is 0720. We met the assault troops on the way in. Due to weather the Germans may not be on the alert. Objective is the Cherbourg Bay. Plan is to cut off the peninsula and take the ports of Le Havre and Cherbourg. A temporary harbour will be made from some eighty old packets (ships) until a harbour is established.' We had seen these old ships plodding along empty, and wondered about it; now we knew! Our assault force consisted of five Divisions of shock troops. Silently we breathed a prayer for those guys that had to get ashore and establish a beachhead in the face of everything the Huns had to throw at them. 'Once the beachhead is established,' the Captain went on, 'it will be a race between us and the Germans to keep supplies coming up, that's all.' We, on board the ship, felt jubilant at the thought of the second front finally starting after all those hard years on the North Atlantic bringing supplies over, building up, just waiting for the day. I myself had spent over four years away from home, with over two dozen crossings to my credit, and there were many more senior ratings aboard ship who held a similar record. There were eight of us in the mess at the time of the Skipper's speech, and miraculously a bottle of rum appeared and we drank a solemn toast to the success of the attack. As the Captain put it, 'We are helping to make history.'

"6 June, 2110 Hours—Captain just finished giving us the lay of the land. Viz.—Six Narvik destroyers and eight submarines have been sighted at 1900 coming along the Ushant peninsula heading up channel. Between us and the enemy are four destroyers, two Polish and two British. Two more are joining them now. Five of the subs are headed in the general direction of the Scilly Isles (our territory). The destroyers are to stop the Narviks. I might add at this juncture that Narviks are the best the enemy has. Five gun turrets (calibre NK), eight torpedoes (fish) and plenty fast. Length 410 feet. Tomorrow is D-Day for us. May God be on our side! The enemy is less than seventy miles away.

"7th of June—Fairly quiet day. Third boiler banked. Went below at 2000 hrs. then things started to happen. Various contacts with subs. One suddenly appeared 100 yards on starboard side! Just the periscope. Immediately a 'Full Ahead', and we opened on it with everything that we could bring to bear, plus depth charges. *Skeena* also opened up! Immediately she (sub) went down again. Four fish were fired, acoustic. One was so close to *Skeena* that the boys thought she was gone. Enemy aircraft also handy. Secured at 2340 hrs.

"8th of June—Below at 0800. Things happen again. Subs fire four fish at our Group. Something wrong! Their fish explode harmlessly. A few counter attacks pulled off with negative results. Aircraft are negative but some enemy aircraft are in the vicinity. Secured at 2340 hrs. Continued to wait for her to surface. Finally surfaced eight miles away. We fired but she dived. Knew she couldn't last much longer, but we were called to intercept four enemy destroyers. Were all ready, but called off again. Meanwhile the sub surfaced in fog and escaped. The Captain said to stand-by to intercept enemy destroyers.

"9th of June—At 0245 the alarm rang and we went toward the enemy. Their fire-power was about 4:1 and some of us were wondering how we'd make out. However, the two F-Class destroyers came around astern of the enemy and opened fire. Salvos were exchanged and one Jerry made off and blew up when he hit a mine. One of our ships was damaged, but the other one chased the enemy until two Canadian Tribals came up. *Haida* and *Huron* scored hits on an enemy destroyer. One of them blew up, apparently from a hit in the magazine. This made two down. The others made off firing over their shoulders. We returned to our regular patrol.

"10th of June—quiet morning watch. The Captain gave details of last night's battle, and stated that there were many subs being sent to cut supplies to the beachhead. At 1445 the gong went again. Sub surfaced two miles away. Up knots and away we go. Standing on the fo'c'sle I see a torpedo wake cut across our bows. The ship went 20 degrees to port and it passed about 25 feet from us. Another was seen on the port side almost simultaneously. Wow! The sub then crash dived and same old stuff with negative results. Away again at 1920 hrs. *Restigouche* dropped ten charges. Negative results. Picked up some fresh fish for the galley. Sighted a 'Wimpy' (Wellington bomber) on the horizon.

"11th of June—Below in the middle watch. **Skeena** spots sub. Negative results. Dammit. In the afternoon, up knots to catch a sub on the surface. Aircraft beat us to it and sank sub. Air support is good today. Oil getting low now. Hell broke out at 2130. Up to 25 knots. The engine room informed me that we were closing two Hun sweepers and to expect anything as you could see the French coast (enemy held). Was relieved at midnight, and action stations broke out at 0150. We did not know what to expect as we were on the enemy's doorstep. But again the enemy beat it and I got to sleep at 0500. We then headed to our base (Plymouth) to replenish our fuel and ammunition. Arrived safely and without incident at 1000 hrs. Afterwards I found out the results of the trip. Subs sunk: 3 by aircraft. Damaged: 1 by my own ship. A new record was made in having acoustic fish fired at us. Ten.

"15 June 2130 hrs, after two days patrol off Land's End—Captain said we are headed out to our old hunting ground tonight. Subs are trying to get through again. One sank the **Mourne** this AM, but was attacked and damaged and is considered to be handy. (AGWL Note: U-boat records claim **Mourne** was sunk 3 May!) Possibility of another one also. Captain said he could not promise us sleep tonight, and it is a good night to wear lifebelts. Gee, and I've got the middle too!

"Wed 5 July 1944, Message to: Escort Group 12 Ships' Companies from Senior Officer EG12. Time 1930—'By the luck of the draw, we are the first to play the new game on the enemy's doorstep. Let us see that we do not throw away what fortune has given us. Good luck.' This signal was accompanied by the pipe: 'Hands will go to night action stations around 2400'. As I write this, I am waiting for the Captain to let us know 'What's in the wind', at 2045.

"Captain has just spoken. 'Tonight we play a new game. Enemy mine sweepers come out of Brest to escort subs in. Subs are on the surface for the last 20 miles. We are to up knots and sweep in across the path of sweepers. No challenging. Anything is cannon food. After we have beaten the sweepers,' the Captain went on matter-of-factly, 'we will carry on after the subs that they were to meet. Nice work! We will be five or six miles off the coast, and if we don't engage the enemy we should be out by about 0230.' He went on to describe the sweepers: 'Main armament is two 4.1 inch guns. See first and shoot first, that's all!' Yes, I'm scared but calm. I've got the middle.

"Thursday, 6 July/44, Alongside at Devonport —Well, it happened! Last night we went to action stations at 2300 hrs. My watch was ordered below so that we would not have to change watches in the middle of an action. Three boilers hooked up. Speed was increased to Full Ahead, and in we went, Hell for Leather, looking for trouble. We found it in the shape of three minesweepers and two subs surfaced, doing 12 knots. They challenged us and our reply was in the shape of a salvo from the big guns. They promptly opened up on us. They raked us with gunfire from stem to stern. Down below, we could hear the hits but everything was OK down there. We let drive with our torpedoes and secured a direct hit on the second ship. It blew up. (AGWL Note: Not so! This was written in the PO mess in the excitement of the day. Senior analysis established that there were no strikes from 18 torpedoes fired.) The third German ship was left blazing. Also got hits on the sub. Score: Two sunk. One by first two salvos, one by torpedo (see above). One possibly sunk, as it was left blazing furiously. Sub damaged by gunfire. Our casualties were eighteen wounded including the Captain, who when wounded refused to leave the bridge. There are quite a few shell holes in the ship. High explosive hits on the bridge, holes in the funnels and ship's side. Damage is only superficial considering the action.

"25 July/44, Somewhere off Cherbourg—Last night at about 2220 hrs the Luftwaffe decided to do something about us calmly patrolling along their coast. As usual, my watch was below as it had been for every other major action we had. Steaming quite peacefully on two boilers at 15 knots. Suddenly a loud explosion and speed is increased to 22 knots! Action stations goes and full speed is rung, about 27 knots. More explosions. I am holding the steam pressure OK until they ring for 30 knots. Then the steam goes back to 210 lb (normally 310). The third boiler stop valves were jammed! Our guns were chattering and banging and the acrid smell of cordite came down the fans.

"Suddenly a loud explosion and we heeled over hard. The blast started the boiler pulsating. One of the stokers dropped to the plates instinctively, while I hung on to the air valve grimly, keeping my eyes on the gauges. The ship straightened up again, and I chalked down 'Near Miss' on our oil heater for the benefit of the stokers, as you couldn't hear yourself speak with the noise of the machinery. Secure went at 2320 hrs. After I got up top I found out what had happened. One enemy plane had come over as a decoy and of course our fighters tore after it. While they were busy, other enemy aircraft came over and launched their glider bombs, or "Chase Me Charlies" as we call them. Six in all were launched. Only one at us, apparently. This was launched about a mile away and at high altitude. It was coming right at us with deadly accuracy. The guns opened up but couldn't stop it. I guess the extra speed plus the manoeuvring saved us, as the bomb hit right in our wake about 200 feet astern of the ship. We were doing about 28 and a half knots at the time, so you can imagine what the extra half knot meant to us. Now we are up channel away from Ushant looking for a couple of subs. Maybe we'll find them.

"11 August/44, 2100 hrs, 3 miles off Ushant—'The Captain will speak over the SRE within the next hour.' The QM has just made this pipe. In a little while we will see what's up. We know we are going in to Brest tonight, as the third boiler is required at 2300 hrs. Captain has just spoken. 'We are to be joined by another ship, HMS Albrighton, at 2300. Then we sweep south to Penmarch Point. There we turn around and sweep up, close to the coast and carry on to Ushant. The Huns are expected to evacuate Brest, and it is possible that they will try to get out tonight. We could see them being pasted by bombers last night and this afternoon. Two destroyers made this run last night and encountered nothing.' The Captain hopes to run into something tonight. We will be close inshore and within easy range of shore batteries. Looks like

I'm on the upper deck for this show. The Skipper was cheered at the end of his speech. I'd hate to be a German tonight!

"12 August/44, Plymouth, 22 hours later.—Here we are, safe in port. This morning we closed up to action stations at 0115 hrs. The moon was a dull red quarter just coming up at the time. Visibility about 1,000 yards, but getting better as the moon rose. There were five of us sweeping at about 22 knots. Suddenly the Skipper said over the SRE 'Three objects close inshore, green six oh, range 6,000 yards.' Being senior ship, we led the others in Line Ahead formation. At about 2,000 yards, our big guns belched out star shells, which were followed by flares and rockets. Two of the enemy were clearly silhouetted on the horizon. Immediately the ships astern of us opened fire with their big guns. The enemy replied as the range closed, but their shells were falling short of us. Now our port Oerlikons opened up, singing their chatter of death and a hoarse cheer rang from a hundred throats as one of the enemy was seen to burst into flames. Then another was hit and promptly laid a smoke screen.

"Our ships circled this smoke, pumping in shells of every size and description. The scene was continually lit up by star shells and flares. When an enemy flare hung over us, it gave one the feeling as walking down the street in the nude. Meanwhile, another enemy ship had caught fire, and these two burning ships headed for the beach where they ran aground. It was then decided to go into the smoke screen to seek the other one. This almost proved fatal to us, as our ships lost formation and **Skeena** came charging straight toward our starboard side at a 90 degree angle. It was a tense moment, but she swerved to port and hit us astern, right in the tiller flats. This put us out of the fight, as it damaged our steering gear and the tiller flat started to flood. All around us the battle was still going on as we rigged up pumps and tried to get our steering gear to function. I was expecting to get shells lobbed at us at any moment, as we were awfully handy to the coast.

"After a while we got going at a slow speed, followed by *Skeena*. Our other ships were still engaging the Hun when I went below at 0410. The fight still carried on for a while, and the shore batteries belched hate at us as we limped towards home at 0530. However, we reached Plymouth without mishap, and even managed to thumb our nose at a tug sent to assist us.

"It is not very clear as yet as to the damage we inflicted on the Hun. We were not hit at all by shells. It appears that three other Huns came along just about the time that we were hit, and our remaining three destroyers engaged them. Seems they sank a couple of these and the one in the smoke screen blew up. That makes five out of commission out of the six. Now we will be out of the war for at least a week anyway. But it is hoped that we are out again in time enough to feel the thrill upon sight of an enemy ship being soundly thrashed."

Editorial comment: The notes by Stoker PO George Stone bring to the page very well the urgency, uncertainty, and excitement of the time. The Boiler and Engine Room ratings were normally in those spaces in action but some, along with miscellaneous other hands, also were in other places below decks. PO

Stone on the 11th August had his Action Station on the foredeck of the ship. On some points in his diary, of course, it must be kept in mind that the Stoker PO Mess was a forcing ground for rumour, being very close to the Chief Stoker who, as noted elsewhere, knew everything even before it happened. With this in mind, the results reported by Stone (as for example on June 11) should be taken with caution.

North by Train

In mid–August many of the crew went north by train while the ship was repaired in the dockyard in Devonport.

By train from Plymouth to Glasgow was interesting in retrospect, but unpleasant in reality, for many stood or sat in a very crowded corridor through the night. British passenger coaches were made up of compartments, each having two facing benches with room for about 4-5 people on each, and with a sliding door to a passageway or corridor along the side of the train. At that time, the trains were absolutely jam-packed with people, and the corridors filled with people and luggage, and almost impassable. Crewe was then an important rail junction and sorting-out point, and usually a change of trains was made there. The large European rail stations generally were made up of a great high shed into which the trains moved on many parallel tracks. Between the train tracks and platforms, and the concourse, was a barrier where the ticket collectors and examiners had their booths, and the Military Police their control points. The concourse itself was also huge, covering the whole width of the tracks, and was a high vaulted structure of steel and glass. Thousands of Navy, Army, and Air Force people struggled doggedly around the Crewe station at night, their awkward duffle bags shouldered and other baggage in hand, "illuminated" by only one small electric light bulb. What could be seen of floor, and signs, and walls, and structure was dim, dingy, dirty, and damaged. Crewe had taken its share of bombs.

The Quality of Leadership

One's joy at being in **Qu'Appelle** knew no bounds in the months following the events recited at the beginning of this chapter. The engine room crew, and the Chief, were enormously pleasing and impressive. They were a great bunch of people. And so too were the wardroom officers. The Commanding Officer, Commander A.M. McKillop, RN, was a leader of men, and was in the course of making the whole of his crew into a band of brothers. When at sea, on each Saturday afternoon, during the dog watches, he met with all the officers in the wardroom for an informal chat and *one* round of drinks. Such a routine, possibly unique, was of great importance to morale in **Qu'Appelle** at that time. The crew, too, thought him a great captain, and one of them wrote later in the ship's newspaper, "Sad beyond words when he left us, To a man we fervently agree, That him we shall always remember, For a Captain of Captains was he". The crew developed this view of their Captain because he spoke to them; every evening he got on the loud speaker and told the crew what had happened and what was going to happen.

With his qualities of leadership, he made himself loved and necessary.

By autumn, however, **Qu'Appelle** had had four captains (and a fifth for a few days as Cmdr C.P. Nixon, RCN, relieved Cmdr Prentice).

After the loss of McKillop, the crew had to subsist almost entirely on rumours and buzzes only; the spirit amongst the officers deteriorated rapidly again, and some felt that the ship had been "ruined" by it as morale fell very low. Morale aboard ship is a rather interesting thing, dependent very strongly on the senior officers, on their respect for the crew, and on their handling of the few amongst the crew who are troublemakers. Those always exist, and they can destroy a ship if the captain and First Lieutenant allow it. As mentioned elsewhere here, Lord Louis Mountbatten in his commands was able to deal with such problems with exquisite ability. But the quality of leadership is not universal, nor found in all installed leaders.

By late autumn part of our trouble arose from the success of the Invasion of Europe, which had made the Atlantic a much safer place, and foreshadowed the coming end of the war. So the ship was full of rumours and buzzes, especially about tying up in Halifax next time. That buzz was with us repeatedly, raising hopes and spirits when it got started, and becoming then especially destructive when it was not fulfilled. There were some who had the view at the time that the First Lieutenant should do something to stop it, but he could not or would not, for he himself was caught up in its toils. No one really knew what the future held. Such a condition is custom-made for the destruction

The Lives of a Seaman, as sketched by Parker in "The H-69."

of morale, and it takes a very special kind of captain and senior staff to combat it.

But with all its bad start and difficulties, the crew of **HMCS** *Qu'Appelle* could be proud of its performance at sea; and leadership qualities were to be found throughout the ship. During the invasion months, various of the crew of the ship earned decorations which they thoroughly deserved—Cmdr McKillop the DSC; Yeoman Bloomfield, Wtr PO Bedard, and AB Masters, the DSM; LtCmdr Palmer the OBE. In addition, ERA Tate, ChSto Patry, StoPO Foley, Able Seaman Hannivan, Lt McCully, and Lt Clarance were all Mentioned in Dispatches. There were undoubtedly many more also deserving but never noticed in the melée of battle.

"The H-69"

Somehow there was a group of ratings in **Qu'Appelle** who understood important things about morale, and they began to do something about it. They set to and produced a ship's newspaper, calling it "The H-69", and four monthly issues were produced, September to December of 1944. Ships' newspapers were not unheard of, but they were also not common at all. Though this one was produced by a simple process on an old Ditto Machine, in purple coloured print, the content was unusually able. In it you will find no spelling errors or grammatical mistakes, or much writing of an adolescent nature. Primarily responsible for it was the Captain's writer, PO Paul Bedard.

One of the writers—"Scandal Hawks", according to the masthead—was LSto Harold McFadyen, RCNVR, tall and of piercing eye, pictured to the right in a drawing by one of his shipmates. McFadyen, like a few of the crew, had a beard, but his was one of a rare red variety. For some people who grew a beard, it came in flaming red, starting at the exact line from which they formerly shaved. Above that line, the hair on their heads was black, or brown, or dark, or fair; below it, they carried red both to port and to starboard!

Because of these men and Cmdr Prentice, *Qu'Appelle* ended the year 1944 as a reasonably happy ship.

In the days long before computer and desktop publishing, "The H-69" managed to apply some present-day principles, with a varied style, good headings, good artwork, imaginative (hand-drawn) display typefaces, and careful work. The four issues the staff produced reflect a deep humanity in the crew as seen by the editors. Those editors did the job for love, got paid no extra for it, got no time off work to do it, just did it for the ship. Some of their words repeat and accentuate those of this author, but others present a different and additional view of the ship and its people.

"Chummy" Prentice, he of the Monocle

"The H-69" was not the only thing responsible for improved morale in *Qu'Appelle*! Commander J. D. Prentice, DSO, DSC and Bar, RN (Ret'd), RCN (Temp), had come to the ship as Captain in mid-September, and it was he who was the instigator of "The H-69". At any rate, his picture was on the cover of the first issue of "The H-69". His handwritten wishes occupied the second page, and set the tone:

"Best wishes to 'The H-69'. May it interest us and make us laugh, and help to pass the time till we all see Canada again, and when the war is over may the old copies remind us of these days which will probably seem to us to have been not so hard when one looks back on them. Good luck and good hunting to **HMCS** *Qu'Appelle* and all who serve in her. (Signed) J.D. Prentice."

Prentice, a Canadian, was a former RN officer who had retired to British Columbia in 1934. At the outbreak of war, he put himself at the disposal

of Canadian Naval Service Headquarters, and came to play an important role in the training of corvette crews during the blackest days of the Atlantic War. Later he was Senior Officer of a group of destroyers during Operation Neptune. By the time he joined *Qu'Appelle*, he had been party to the sinking of four U-boats (U621, U678, U984, U501). He was a captain to respect, and well-endowed with the leadership qualities which all could recognize.

Even sixty years after the event, the dominating and powerful leadership of Cmdr Prentice is remembered by matelots in another ship, **HMCS** *Skeena*. Coming alongside one day for some legitimate purpose, the crews of both ships found occasion for fun in the way of a heated exchange of potatoes fired across the narrowing gap. No harm was done, but the next time a similar opportunity offered, *Skeena's* crew heard, and obeyed, a peremptory voice from *Qu'Appelle's* bridge, in a fine English accent, carried across the gap from a loud hailer in Prentice's hand, "Hello *Skeena*! We will have no potatoes shied this way today!" He had earlier ordered his own crew to have no more of that kind of fun. And not a potato was exchanged.

The first issue of "The H-69", surprisingly, put forth the views of the crew about him, under the heading "Commander Prentice 'Goes Over'." Here's the syrup that followed:

"I like the new Skipper. I like his style; I like his humour; I like his experience; I even like his monocle. I don't like his red mittens, but that doesn't matter.

"He rather surprised the ship's company by calling Church Party at sea last Sunday, but as the service wore on, his motive became obvious. He wished to have a look at us as a body, and he wished to introduce himself.

"Re—the latter, he had a job on his hands which he proved himself well capable of handling. He had to introduce himself to his new ship's company, and at the same time create a favourable impression.

"An officer is 'on the spot' when he is appointed CO to a strange ship. If he has his head screwed on properly he realizes that, to a major extent, the future happiness and efficiency of his crew will depend on the initial impression it receives of him. By that token it is his duty to 'sell' himself favourably. On the other hand, he is obliged to remain within the boundary of Naval reserve. It isn't easy to acquaint himself with a body of naturally suspicious men without coming down off that enforced pedestal of reserve. Ask a Skipper some time!

"Enough then that Cmdr Prentice gave us the decided impression that he knows the score, and that he'll supply the cheese if we supply the bread.

"His observations of us were, I think, sincere. To quote him in essence:- 'I like your attitude. I like your appearance, and I like your experience.'

"Liking, then, seems quite a mutual sentiment!"

I called that "syrup" unfairly, for I know it was meant wholeheartedly.

Adoration by the crew, and the weighting down of his uniform jacket by the authorities with medals did not save Prentice from censure by those very same authorities. Soon after he had assumed command of **Qu'Appelle**, the ship lay at anchor in Loch Foyle awaiting departure for patrol off Iceland. It was to be a sad patrol, but before it had even started, Prentice's ship had a minor disaster to deal with. His ship went aground.

SubLt Vince Murphy was on watch on the bridge at the time, the most junior of the watchkeeping officers in the ship. Seeing that the anchor was dragging, he immediately called the First Lieutenant to tell him so —and found a total lack of interest on his part.

The First Lieutenant's cavalier disregard of his watchkeeper's warning led to a delay of two days in departure on patrol, and to official censure of his disregard—("...incurred the displeasure of the Department of National Defence..."). The delay was caused by the need to visit a dry dock in Belfast for examination of the bottom of the ship for damage, and repairs to the propeller.

The censure spread. The Commanding Officer in a ship bears ultimate responsibility for all things in his command, whether reasonably or not, and Commander Prentice, notwithstanding his DSO, DSC and Bar, shared in the censure of his First Lieutenant. In fact, in the list of those censured for the incident, he stood first and his erring First Lieutenant stood second.

As **Qu'Appelle** left for patrol, another Commanding Officer in her group also moved inexorably closer to judgment for another grounding, one with far more dire consequences, that of **HMCS Skeena**, in quite different circumstances, in far-off Iceland.

Peril to U-Boats! EG12 on Operation Neptune.
From the deck of **HMCS Qu'Appelle**,
English Channel, summer of 1944,
Photographed by Stoker Martyn Harper
HMCS Saskatchewan *(LtCmdr A. Easton, DSC, RCNR),*
HMCS Skeena *(LtCmdr P.F.X. Russel, DSC, RCN),*
HMCS Restigouche *(LtCmdr D.W. Groos, RCN)*

BATTLE HONOURS
Carried by **HMS Foxhound***:*
Basque Roads, 1809, Dardanelles 1915, Atlantic 1939–1941.
Carried by **HMCS Qu'Appelle***:*
Atlantic 1944, Normandy 1944, Biscay 1944

The story is continued from the end of Chapter 2.

... The far sails glimmer, the faint hull grows,
Far-off, but enough; he knows
The rolling lines of a merchant ship.
The wild yell leaps to his idiot lip:
"Ai-yi-aily-!"
Thunderous cries
From the decks below to his eyrie rise;
The old mad lusts of the looters burn.
As one, all eyes to the swaying peak turn
Where he leaps and whirls (to his custom loyal)
In a perilous dance at the far main-royal. ...

The story is continued at the end of Chapter 4.

4. The Stranding of HMCS Skeena

Though headlong wind and heaping tide
Make us their sport tonight,
By force of weather, not of war,
In jeopardy we steer:
"A Song in Storm" R. Kipling

HIS MAJESTY'S CANADIAN SHIP SKEENA, PROUDLY COMMISSIONED IN 1931 in Portsmouth, England, was lost ignominiously thirteen years later on the rocks at Reykjavik, Iceland. *Skeena* was one of the first two warships built to Canadian order, and became the pride of the very small Canadian naval service in the thirties. She was one of only two destroyers, a number of much lesser craft, and a few thousand men in that service when Hitler came to power in Germany.

Technically, **HMCS *Skeena*** belonged to the Royal Navy's "A" Class of destroyers, conceived and designed in the late 1920s. She displaced 1,337 tons on a length of 320 ft, and carried four 4.7 inch guns and two sets of four 21 inch torpedo tubes at launching. Early in the war, her heavy guns were reduced to two, her torpedoes to four. Anti-aircraft guns and anti-submarine weapons were added, and *Skeena* spent the war years almost entirely in anti-submarine activities, with a crew of over 200 men.

Canada had four classes of destroyers in action in the Second World War, River (14 vessels), Town (8),

Tribal (4), and V (2). The last two were heavy and large vessels, launched late in the war, and were the only ones engaged solely in typical "destroyer" missions—fast-moving surface actions against larger vessels. The Town Class was made up entirely of former US four-stackers laid down in 1918; they were part of the WWII exchange of US destroyers for British bases, came into service (mostly) late in 1940, and were engaged entirely in the war against U-boats. The River Class, to which *Skeena* belonged, counted two ships that were Canadian from their launching, but was otherwise a motley group of former Royal Navy vessels, transferred into Canadian service at various times during the War. They all dated from the early thirties, and were all similar in size, speed, and armament. They were all engaged primarily in escort service in the Atlantic.

For a few months in 1944, however, various of the River Class destroyers, including *Skeena*, joined with the heavier Tribals and Vs out of Plymouth on various missions directly associated with Operation Neptune, the invasion of Fortress Europe. Some of these were destroyer missions, and presented the only opportunities in the whole Canadian wartime service of the River Class for the discharge of torpedoes.

At Sea Near Iceland, the year 1944, on October 25

By September of 1944, the waters around France had become much safer with the capture by the Allied armies of the ports on the Bay of Biscay, and the withdrawal of the submarines to German and

Norwegian ports. To block access to the Atlantic from those ports, the ships under Commander Prentice as Senior Officer (**Qu'Appelle**, **Skeena**, **Chaudiere**, **St Laurent**) were assigned to an area towards Iceland, and found themselves there one day in October in a most tremendous gale, with mountainous seas.

One does not expect halcyon days at sea, in general, of course, though they are taken with gratitude when they do come. But in October and later in the waters around Iceland, they probably never come. By January and February the weather in those waters is unbelievably terrible, as many ships found, ice piled thick on decks and superstructures. But this day in October presented no such problems. Just the seas and the wind and the squalls. The sun

The Cook at Sea, according to "The H-69"

shines pallidly, and sea birds glide effortlessly here and there. Then a black cloud stretching down to the water slowly approaches, and suddenly the wind is shrieking, and hail streaks horizontally over the deck. The seascape is shot with black sheets of hail and rain, and the various planes of the distant waves are picked out in lightening shades of greys. It is a beautiful wild sight as the sun again breaks out.

Enjoying the awe-inspiring sight of the waves and the fury, the Doctor (Max Frost), the Chief Engineer (Jim Palmer), and I stood for a while in the protection of the canopy over the engine room access hatches.

Standing there, with our feet covering one of the joints between deck plates, we could feel those plates moving against each other as the ship and its deck worked and distorted in the maelstrom of waves. Barely able to hold our position, we watched the waves board the side of the vessel and sweep astern with a roar. That is, we watched until, in the increasing violence, one of those boarding seas swept over our position too and soaked us all. That was the wildest time I ever saw at sea, and at times I feared that the ship would not recover from her roll but would go right over. Ships were actually lost in the Pacific by rolling over. That night at dinner, the "fiddle" itself (a divider on the table top designed to keep things more or less in place in rough weather), the contents of the table, and a steward or two shot incontinently across the wardroom, and in the ship's galley the Chief Cook had all the soup spilled over himself. The table was abandoned as an eating place!

At risk in the violence of the weather conditions, Prentice was ordered by the shore authorities to run for Reykjavik, and instructed each of his group to anchor independently in a "lee" to the eastward of Engey Island in Reykjavik harbour. I put lee in quotation marks, for the wind was not only tremendous, but it veered back and forth and round and about, so that there was no real lee at all. The Commanding Officer and Navigator of *Skeena* voiced doubts to each other about the wisdom of going to anchor, preferring to stay at sea, but said nothing to their Senior Officer. They and we came to anchor late in the evening, and steaming watches were maintained in the engine room, ready for any emergency arising from the dragging of the anchor. About two in the morning, Paul Savard, the Second Lieutenant and my cabin mate, came off watch, and climbing into his bunk told me that **Skeena** had dragged and had gone on the rocks.

On board **Skeena** that night.

I was not on board **Skeena** and cannot report at first-hand the conditions experienced by those who were. But those conditions and the events on board **Skeena** that night are pallidly reflected in the proceedings of the Board of Enquiry convened to look into her loss, convened not long after to sit on board **HMS** *Baldur* not far away from the wreck. *Baldur* was an old vessel that served as the local command in Iceland. There sat Commander C. Parker, RN (Ret'd), of **HMS** *Baldur*, Acting LtCmdr C. Nixon, RCN, of **HMCS** *Chaudiere*, and ActLtCmdr R. Barr, RNVR, of **HMS** *Baldur*. They sat over a three day period and listened to a dozen or more witnesses to the disaster. The questions they were interested in were "How Did It Happen?" and "Who Was Responsible?" For those involved from **Skeena** the Enquiry no doubt was a nightmare.

But the nightmare started on the night of October 25.

'Stop,' they rang down from the bridge to the Engine Room, when the ship had come to her anchor. 'Stop,' the telegraph said, but by voice it was added, "Carry on at Immediate Notice For Steam; don't go away!" Had the bridge been finished with the engines, they would have rung down 'Finished with Engines', and the engine room people would then have known that they could act as though in harbour, safely alongside a dock. But 'Immediate Notice For Steam' said the bridge, knowing that the engines might be needed at any moment to deal with a dragging anchor and to avoid the disastrous and dreadful rocks off to the lee. And in the engine room the watch continued as if they were still at sea. The telegraph from the bridge was silent, standing mutely at Stop, but steam stood ready behind the throttles from two boilers, ready at 250 pounds per square inch to flood into the engines at a moment's notice.

On the bridge and on the deck, earlier, the Captain and his officers and his crew had crept into the channel between Engey and Videy Islands. Told earlier, in the maelstrom, by the Senior Officer, to anchor independently, they anxiously perused the charts, voicing no objections, and to anchor they came, the starboard anchor veered to five shackles, and the port anchor ready to let go. There was only one anchor windlass on the foredeck, and the starboard anchor cable occupied it; to let go the port anchor would have meant fifteen minutes of work in removing the starboard cable from the windlass and its replacement with the port cable. More of a consideration than this immediate work, they said afterwards to a doubtful Board of Enquiry, was the worry that, should it be necessary to weigh anchor, the fifteen minutes would be required again in a reverse of the procedure. So there hung the port anchor, ready, but not in the water. That only one anchor lay set in the bottom was, in fact, almost an invitation to disaster on such a night.

And the bottom was not good for anchoring. Everyone knew it. An anchor must bite into the bottom, and dig in, and become one with the bottom if a ship is to hang safely on it. If the bottom is rocky, or stony, or even sandy sometimes, then, oh then? Sometimes, and for some purposes, such bottoms are enough. But in storm conditions, with extreme and gusty winds, and with passing squalls of sleet and hail to obscure the vision of the watch on deck, then, oh then? In the engine room and the boiler room, with its two boilers, the watch had little to do but idle away the time while paying attention only to minor matters. They could feel the ship shift and shake with the wind, but felt no concern. In the various messes, those off watch slept thankfully after a rough day.

But what of the watch on deck? Having come to the place for anchoring, the officers on the bridge look around for lights and landmarks, and measure the angle of several of them on the compass. As the anchor holds, and the ship strains against the anchor cable, they measure those angles again and enter them in the log. Measure them and hug them and treasure them. Measure them and worry repeatedly about them, and measure again. On a dark night life and death hang on the numbers, for only by recognizing that the angles are changing can a ship's managers know that the anchor is not holding. The Captain was on the bridge with his Navigating Officer, his "Pilot", and listened intently to the numbers, Engey Light, Flashing Red and Green every five seconds, bore 276,

Engey Reef Buoy, Flashing Red every 3 seconds, bore 210, Langarnes Spit Buoy, Flashing every five seconds, bore 155. And ominously astern, the dark loom of Videy Island confirmed the threat from all around. They watched and measured and re-measured until satisfied that all was stable. The ship seemed secure on its one anchor, though embedded in a bottom that was itself far from secure.

"Now," said the Captain, "now, we must have a full anchor watch. Pilot, you do understand those bearings, do you not? Yes, a full anchor watch. We'll have the cable party on the forecastle, we'll have the quartermaster and a hand to man the telegraph in the wheelhouse, we'll have the Officer of the Watch on the bridge, and we'll have two boilers under steam, Chief, two boilers at Immediate Notice for Steam. Now, then, Pilot, you do understand the terrible significance of those bearings, do you? I'm going to leave you as the Officer of the Watch on the bridge, for you and No. 1, of all my officers, are the most reliable and the most experienced. No. 1 is to be your relief when the time comes. We have left the starboard cable on the capstan, it is not taken to the bitts, so that it will be easier to work should we have the terrible misfortune to drag. Call me immediately if anything changes. *Immediately!*"

Dog-tired from a full day and more of worry and concern, assured now that the ship was safely at anchor, and that the bridge watch was alert to the dangers and the needs, the Captain retired for rest, well after midnight, and sank into a deep sleep in his cabin in the after section of the ship. It lasted but an hour.

On the foredeck the cable party felt the blast of the bitter wind and huddled against it in the shelter of A-gun shield. In the various messes those off watch slept thankfully after a rough day.

On the bridge, the Navigating Officer checked the vital bearings once more, and turned the watch over to the First Lieutenant, to No. 1, to the second in command of the ship, and retired in turn for a well-earned rest, first telling the Captain that all was well. No. 1 in turn began his routine of checking the bearings, every five minutes, with heavy flurries of hail obscuring his vision from time to time. The ship, he later said, was yawing or swinging less than 10 degrees; had it been more, he might have thought the anchor would be worried out of the bottom. But as one obscuring flurry thinned around the ship, to his horrified vision it was indeed evident that the precious bearings had changed, the ship was moving, moving fast, and moving towards land. The engines! the engines!—and the telegraph to the engine room rang frantically. There, the men on watch opened the throttles, opened them quickly, opened them for a speed of twelve knots, then for fifteen, and then for Full Ahead. And she touched, she juddered, she took the ground. In the engine room they felt it first, heard the first knocking, the first damaging blows to the screws, and looked at each other with wild surmise. No.1 had the Captain called and rushed off to see to the gear on the forecastle, the anchoring gear that they had all been so dependent on.

Into the Captain's rest, into his sleep, into his life, intruded a wild call and an insistent jarring, a knocking, a roughness of movement that was not of the sea, a horror of realization. Off again to the bridge he rushed. And there he heard the confirmation of disaster. The ship, he saw, had dragged astern onto the rocks off Videy Island, and disaster was upon them.

"Half ahead both," he cried. "Half ahead both," and the telegraph hand in the wheelhouse responded immediately, but in the engine room they could feel only the crude vibrations of a damaged screw damaging itself further. Too late, too late! "Full ahead both," he cried, and down the chain the order passed, but to open the steam valves further was obviously to no avail as the noise from the stern hammered in their ears. The engineers closed the throttles for the last time, and could respond no more to the telegraph, as she was bumped aft, bumped and lurched sickeningly as the waves bore down on her.

"Set the Port anchor." The Captain ordered. "Where's No 1? Where is he?" On the forecastle, No 1, in a fever of concern, got the port anchor ready to let go, and slipped it. On the bridge, the Captain struggled with chaos. "Send a signal, send a signal that we need help!" "Send it now!" "Don't wait!" "Get the ship's company on deck, get them up!" "No 1, get them up!" "Get your men up from the machinery spaces, Chief. Get them up now. Now!"

And in the boiler room, the stokers prepared to abandon their posts, shutting down the fires for the last time, staring in horror at the deck plates being jolted out of place by rocks pushing up from the bilges. By rocks, my god! Ready to climb the ladders out of his now-useless domain, LSto Don German opened the steam relief valves, and the boilers began to empty themselves of their dangerous contents.

"What? What's that you say?" "Close all watertight doors and hatches, close those doors." "Over with the Carley floats, over they go on the lee side, on the lee side, on the side the waves are not sweeping." "Get the primers out of the depth charges, get them out. We mustn't have depth charges exploding in the water should we go down." "Prepare to tow forward, No 1, get the lines ready on the fo'c'sle, get them ready!" "What's the damage, Chief, let me know." On the bridge the telegraph stood mutely at Half Ahead, vainly, and for ever.

"We've broached, we're broadside-to, tell that trawler to lay off, come no closer, leave us be, for he can do no good now. We've broached, we're broadside to." "Get lines at each end of all those Carley floats. Tail them. They've got to reach the beach and let us haul them back aboard. Tail them!" "Stand by Carley floats and rafts!" "Flooded forward, you say, Chief? Flooded forward? Flooded as far back as the Engine Room? My God! She's in danger of breaking in two, breaking in two, and capsizing? Abandon ship! Abandon ship! Away all rafts! Abandon ship!"

As I write, the noise is of my keyboard tapping gently, and of muted sounds from the remainder of the house, all being calm and still. What is written is a faint reflection of the reality of a disaster, in which noise and cold and fear were dominant. On board **Skeena**, the noise of the wind and the seas was overwhelming, of seas breaking over the windward side of the vessel, of men shouting and calling, of orders half heard in the din, of the overwhelming roar of steam at high pressure venting to the winds, even of the ship's siren and, terribly, of the harsh tearing of rocks at the thin and fragile steel of the ship's structure as she lurched and shuddered to the incoming seas.

"Abandon ship!"—the ultimate order in the midst of chaos. In that chaos and the confusion of noise and wind and water, maybe what was said was only, "Prepare to abandon ship!" But they went, they went, one—two—three. The beach was but fifty yards away, but in the fierce winds and vicious currents and confusion, one raft overturned, and one was swept away when its line broke, and only one reached shore. The Captain saw it, watching with horror over the side of the bridge. To send more was madness, and the order to Abandon Ship was cancelled, with water and oil from damaged tanks sweeping the length of the deck and cascading into the bridge as waves broke their fury and power on her. "Stop Abandoning Ship! Stop Abandoning Ship!!" The nightmare was in full swing, for those left aboard and for the few who had got ashore in the bitter cold and dark.

"All hands for'ard! Clear the after section of the ship! All hands for'ard!!" "No smoking in the Mess Decks! No smoking on the Upper Deck!!" "No smoking. No smoking!!" The odour of fuel oil was strong in the air, a stench in the nostrils, a threat in the pit of the stomach. "No smoking in the ship!!" "Rig scrambling nets and lifelines on the port side. Scrambling nets and lifelines to the port side!!" "All hands clear the Upper Deck. All hands clear the Upper Deck!!" The stern of the stricken ship lurched drunkenly as the breakers rolled into her, rolled in and broke over her, rolled in and threatened to break her in two.

"Away No. 2 whaler! Away No. 2 whaler!! We"ve got to get a line ashore. Get a line ashore!" But in the seas and the dark, the fragile boat lasted only a moment, and was smashed into matchwood in the water. And so they waited, helpless to do more, waited for light, waited for help to arrive on the desolate island, waited for the shore authorities to pluck them out of their nightmare. At last, in the murk of the morning, those shore authorities were able to do so, and the final order to Abandon Ship was made. All remaining on board managed to reach the stability of Videy Island, but fifteen of those who had tried to do so in the dark and confusion of the night were gone for ever.

Reykjavik

Next morning, **Skeena** was a sorry sight, broadside-to and offshore by a few dozen feet, listing, desolate, dead.

At some point that morning salvage of 'things' from **Skeena** was decided on, and the Senior Engineers of **Skeena** and **Qu'Appelle** were with the party that went aboard. **Skeena** was a sad sight, covered with fuel oil, flooded compartments, a waterlogged engine room, and a welter of lines and abandoned gear. And the engine room telegraph on the bridge standing still at Half Ahead. Of course, much was saved but in comparison with the vessel itself, it was nothing. The hulk was sold for scrap a year later.

Another event of profound impact was the funeral

HMCS *Skeena* *aground on the rocks of Videy Island, Iceland, in a photograph to be found in the archival records of the Board of Enquiry into her stranding, held October 1944 RCN NU*

of those who had died in the attempt to reach land, the most elaborate military funeral held in Iceland to that time with all the services taking part. The most vivid memory attached to it is of one of the three Chaplains, his mane of red hair blowing in the eternal wind of Iceland, and the wild extent of the fiord far off behind his back away down the hill. Parties from all the ships lined up solemnly and unhappily, the sun fitful with passing cloud and scud, the gravestones all about, and their comrades in a row of fifteen caskets

at their feet. Years later the Minister at the church the author attended in Toronto, the Reverend Dr. Richard Davidson, somehow mentioned Iceland, and it turned out that he was the very person who had conducted that funeral service, and whose red mane blew in the Iceland winds. He was the Padre for the RCAF in Reykjavik. Years later, Claire and I walking near the harbour one day found the wind was overwhelming, enough to blow one off one's feet! In the cemetery, the inscriptions on some of the stones of the many young men left there by the war are heart-rending; "To know him was to love him", said one. It speaks for all.

Naturally, **Qu'Appelle**'s crew had leave in Reykjavik with its blond people, painted buildings, tidiness, maritime ambience and narrow streets.

Meanwhile, starting less than 48 hours after the loss of the vessel, the Board of Enquiry began its sittings; the senior of the three officers sitting in judgment was Royal Navy. In **HMS *Baldur*** during those sittings they were comfortable, warm, secure, safe, quiet, and unaffected by any confusion or by any maelstrom of waves and wind and hail and urgent deadly worry. The Board sat, and issued its findings promptly. It found serious fault in some areas and with some people, and no fault in other areas and with other people. It is possible that those findings damaged the careers of some of the people. But the lasting damage was that which arose on the night of October 25, in the year 1944, arose and struck down a fine ship and fifteen of her great people, and seared the lives of many others.

A Minor Glossary

A few words in this chapter may need some explanation for some:

Bearings	The angles measured off the ship between objects and the fixed north line seen on the compass.
Bitts	The firmly-fixed "knobs" on a ship's deck to which lines can be made fast.

Cable	The anchor line (in this case).
Capstan	The windlass around which cable is wrapped to recover it back to the ship, driven by steam or by electricity.
Carley floats or rafts	A form of life-raft carried by ships, much less subject to damage than boats, and specifically designed for life-saving purposes.
Fo'c'sle	The forward part of the ship, especially the upper deck.
Half Ahead	An order to the Engine Room to set the throttles on the engines at half power.
Lee	The side of a ship or an island on which the wind is not blowing. The lee of an island is calm as compared with the windward side.
Log	The notebook on the bridge into which important things having to do with the ship's movements and safety are entered.
Primers	Part of the firing mechanism in an explosive weapon.
Quarter-master	Senior hand at the steering position.
Scrambling nets	Nets with about an 8 inch mesh hung on the side of a ship in case of need, which men in the water could easily grasp, and up which they might climb.
Signal	A message sent by radio or light or semaphore or other means.
Veered	Let go, in relation to the part of the anchor cable between the ship and its anchor.

Whaler   The ship's boat, designed for passage from one spot to another, usually under power of oars, but not commonly for life-saving in tumbled and broken waters, though Captain Bligh made his epic passage in such a ship's boat.

The story is continued from the end of Chapter 3.

They cheer him on in the perilous maze
That had brought them luck through their savage days,
Had marked each prize for murder and flame
And led them on to their lurid fame.

The story is continued at the end of Chapter 5.

5. HMCS WARRIOR

Gawd bless this world! Whatever she 'ath done—
Excep' when awful long—I've found it good.
So write, before I die, "E liked it all'
"A Song in Storm" R. Kipling

THE PLANNERS AND SENIOR PEOPLE OF THE ROYAL
CANADIAN NAVY THROUGH THE EARLY 1940S considered
that the only real kind of navy, the only one worth
having, was a big-ship navy, with cruisers and destroyers
that could take part in big-ship battles. With reluctance
they built a small-ship navy out of corvettes and
minesweepers, with a dozen and a half destroyers to
keep some semblance of real-navy about it all. Officers
of the permanent force, the RCN, were mostly able
to avoid the small ships that by ensuring the flow of
supplies to Britain brought about the end of Nazism.
With the coming end of the war in Europe and in the
Atlantic Ocean it was obvious that the senior people
were at least partially right, and there would be no
place or need for small ships in the war against Japan
in the Pacific Ocean. It was also obvious that the new
navies of the world would be built around aircraft and
their carriers, armed with rocket weapons. In 1944,
with that day approaching fast, Canada contracted for
a position in the building of aircraft carriers in Britain.
HMCS *Warrior* was the first of them; she was laid
down in 1944 in Harland and Wolff shipyard in Belfast

and her construction was well advanced by mid 1945. There was to be an intersection of her career with that of the author. But first, Boiler Water had some claims to make, and that brought **HMCS *Protector*** into the picture.

The Commander of the base at Sydney, HMCS ***Protector***, was a firm believer in recreation and sports in his endless struggle against personnel trouble. He instituted and promoted all sorts of games, night classes in the schoolhouse, hobby shops, rifle range, and so on; all were well-used. No one complained of a draft to ***Protector***, despite its being eight miles out of town and a small town at that. The happy state of mind was palpable in the base. Would that all leaders of men could be as perceptive as that base commander, who belonged as one in a fraternity with McKillop and Prentice, with Patry and Dauphinee, and with many others in ***Qu'Appelle***.

Things were not so happy in Halifax (as the riots soon to erupt on VE–Day were to demonstrate), nor in the Boiler Water office. There were now nine people in it—nine people, though one alone could do in an

"Hobby Lobby", *a cartoon from a contemporary service newspaper in* **HMCS *Protector***

hour or two all the work that had to be done. They all saw the same thing, and the place was a hotbed of resentment and complaint. (There had actually been a strike in January!) But the author's days of Boiler Water were close to an end. About April 12 in 1945 there were orders to join an RN ship, an aircraft carrier, for training in Rosyth, Scotland. The objective was more training to allow appointment to **HMCS** *Warrior*, then a'building in Belfast, and intended for the Far East. Jim Palmer had a hand in arranging this, for he had been "sowing seeds".

SS *Volendam* soon had a new passenger bound for Liverpool, and thence to Edinburgh and Rosyth, the Royal Navy dockyard where lay **HMS** *Battler*.

HMS *Battler*

The aircraft carrier *Battler* in mid-1945 was engaged in activities aimed at Japan, training RAF pilots out of Rosyth, near Queensferry at the north end of the Forth Bridge. The Forth Bridge is one of the world's very famous structures, and was pictured on one of the Meccano Set boxes common in the 1930s. A train passed over it every five or six minutes, looking very small and toylike.

Battler lay at anchor near the bridge on most nights, and during the day sailed off into the Firth of Forth, carrying aircraft and flight crews who took off and landed repeatedly. Though fun to watch, the flying

from such a pocket handkerchief of a deck was very sobering indeed. Even seasoned pilots misjudged their position, and some went into the water. One did so after passing over our head as we stood on a sponson at the side of the ship—and the pilot, who had over a thousand hours in his logbook, seemed to take forever to come to the surface.

Some of the watching had in it elements of the Four Stooges. One day four of us were standing on the catwalk at the end of the ship approached by incoming aircraft, and just about four feet below the landing deck. As the first of the day's aircraft came for a landing, he was waved off at the very last moment and the four of us got jammed in the door we had been standing by as the aircraft passed two feet above our heads.

The flight-deck personnel had no convenient door to duck through, and had to face the danger squarely. Aircraft landing on to the deck were intended to be arrested by catching a hook on arrestor wires strung from one side of the deck to the other. Though there were several arrestor wires, sometimes all were missed, and an aircraft then stood in danger of scooting off the other end of the deck into the water in the path of the oncoming ship. To prevent that unhappy circumstance (most of the time anyway!), there were two 'barriers' downstream of the arrestor-wires, the barriers consisting of another kind of wire, each barrier manned by four crew, two at each end. They had to raise the barrier in case of need, and quickly get out any pilot who ran into it, anticipating that there might be a fire. The four men on the port side were especially vulnerable, for almost all pilots veered toward their port side, steering away from the massive obstacle of the bridge structure to their starboard side which acted psychologically in pushing them to port.

Most pilots who got into trouble were lucky, and relatively unscathed. Their luck was not everlasting, though, for one who walked away from hitting a gun in the ship got a severed spinal cord the next day landing on an airfield ashore.

HMS *Battler* was built in the United States, and was on loan to the RN. Even for the most highly experienced amongst the crew the engine room was a strange place, for the boilers were in the same space as the engines, and energy efficiency had been the watchword during her design. In **Qu'Appelle** there had been drain lines blowing to the atmosphere everywhere—little drifts and jets of steam or of hot water, in amounts thought at the time of her design to be too minor to save. But in **Battler** there was nothing of the kind. No least bit of used steam or warm water was wasted; it all went to preheating the boiler feed water. A particularly interesting point of design had to do with the final heating of boiler feed water. In RN ships, it was (always?) done in a closed heater, with steam on one side of tubes and the water on the other. In the US-built **Battler**, the water was brought into direct contact, at almost two-thirds of an atmosphere of vacuum, with exhaust steam from the auxiliary engines. One great advantage of such a system is that air is caused to escape from the water as it heats, so reducing the amount of corrosive oxygen introduced to the boilers. In **Battler** this was especially important for the boilers operated at the high temperature of 450° F. The drawback to the direct heating of feed water had to do with the need to keep sufficient pressure on the suction end of the boiler feed water pumps; this meant putting a feed-water tank away up above, in the aircraft hangar, which seemed to us to be a particularly vulnerable location for such an important service. A major fire or explosion in the hangar could easily deprive the boilers of water and the engines of power.

Not all ships built in the USA were superior to those of the Royal Navy. Bob Brooks of the Class of 4T3 Engineering became Engineer Officer in what turned out to be a 'horror'. Early in the war standing alone against Germany and its U-boat threat the British Commonwealth was desperately short of ships to put to sea against that threat. Meanwhile, the USA had many old destroyers which might be useful, and a deal was made whereby fifty of them were given in exchange for long-term rights to the use of bases here and there around the Atlantic. The ships had been built at the end of WWI, and soon after building became the subject of a serious investigation into their many deficiencies in design and construction when compared with new British ships. To add to their inherent deficiencies they had suffered through many years of storage until removal for delivery to the RN. The US Navy did its utmost to put the ships into acceptable shape, but could remedy few of the many problems. Canada was given eight of the ships, designated as Town Class. It turned out that our Town Class destroyers were full of mechanical problems—

endless steering failures, leakage of sea water into fuel tanks, engine breakdowns, boiler problems; in short, they were nightmares. In addition they were subject to serious storm damage, making them inherently unsuited to the North Atlantic. Brooks experienced all of these conditions in **HMCS *Annapolis***. ***Battler***, however, had no such problems.

Later, **HMCS *Warrior***, a'building in Belfast, was found to be totally unlike ***Battler***, and time spent in the latter had been essentially wasted. One important insight developed, in it, however—namely, that corrosion and rusting were worse causes of equipment malfunction than mechanical failure, and should have much more attention in design.

HMCS *Warrior*

Joining ***Warrior*** in the builder's yard in Belfast, the author was appointed Double Bottoms Officer, who would eventually be presumed to know everything about the closed compartments between the outside hull and the inside shell, and about the pipe lines running near them and about their drainage, etc. Night time was a surprise in Belfast, for the city was lighted by gas with a very few mercury arc lamps here and there. The gas lamps were controlled by clockworks in each,

*A view of the author in full working dress on board **Battler**. The object in the left hand is a wheel wrench, used for opening and closing valves.*

and the upkeep and maintenance expense must have been extraordinary. Going to the Harland and Wolff shipyard was a matter of taking the trolley across Belfast through the downtown section and out to the docks. To be in a Harland and Wolff shipyard was a great pleasure for the new DB officer, for it was at Harland and Wolff in Glasgow that my father had apprenticed as a machinist/toolmaker.

But all interest in being in Belfast at all was soon to evaporate totally for the war against Japan ended abruptly in August. The end of the war was brought about by the Atomic Bomb. In our first year of university Professor Breckenridge told us one day of the great new finding in Germany that the uranium atom could be split by neutrons. Not long after his telling us about it, all news of it dried up, and we heard no more. But when the staggering story of the Hiroshima bomb burst on the world, the professor's description of those first reports from Germany five years earlier was passed on to the officers in *Warrior* as an explanation of how the atom bomb had come about. They wouldn't believe a word of it.

In celebration of the ending of the war several of those officers from *Warrior* in Belfast decided to bicycle to Dublin, and did so late in August, out of uniform. Belfast was not as austere as England and we greedily filled ourselves in Dublin with unfamiliar taste treats—ice cream, milkshakes, coffee, cakes, and goodies generally. We also marvelled at the bicycles in the city. It seemed that almost everyone there had one. And fortunate it was for those that did for the only other vehicular movement was that of buses; as for everything else, the queues for buses were three deep and blocks long. Though we were mostly made welcome, it didn't happen everywhere, and we had one stone thrown at us while walking in Drogheda early one morning outside a church!

But the war was over indeed and with it all interest in the Navy. A very serious allergic rash and scab on the wrists, experienced off-and-on for almost a year, was now useful to move things along in the direction of being elsewhere. The condition, called 'Uniform Dermatitis', was an allergic rash that wept at times, and was extremely uncomfortable, especially in the warmth of an engine room. The last of the doctors to examine the rash said discharge was clearly needed and followed that comment with "You lucky dog!" Over the very strong objections of Commander Fife, Chief Engineer in *Warrior*, it came about.

The first step towards discharge was a move to the Naval Barracks in the manning establishment at **HMCS Niobe**, Greenock. At the time, being critical of the Service in letters home was definitely frowned upon, but comment on *Niobe* could not be avoided. It was established in what had been an asylum for the insane. Seen from a distance, it was a place of great beauty, a fairytale building, a great rich chateau set nestling in the green green hills under a sky of azure blue. Of red sandstone, it was beautifully weathered and its towers and wings and courtyards contrasted wonderfully with the wet and verdant green of the hills. It was a perfect picture. Like many beautiful people, however, it was dreadful inside, though probably not so bad as when it had been used as an asylum for civil matters. Rooms and halls were bare and cheerless, dull, chill, lacking in anything to speak of man's place of grace in the world. There seemed to be a consensus amongst those in it that it was, in fact, still an asylum for the insane

ex Sto. D. German

or, at least, that one had to be insane to wish to be there at all! During the depths of the Battle of the Atlantic, **Niobe** had a cheerless and desperate task in the maintenance of crews in Canadian ships based in the U.K.

Now things moved reasonably quickly, and in due course **HMCS Puncher**, too, had a new passenger, a passenger who was soon enough home and discharged, on the 6th day of November of 1945. Hurrah!

The next spring one of Canada's new ships of the coming big-ship Navy visited Montreal. She was the aircraft carrier **HMCS Magnificent**. **Warrior** had been exchanged for **Magnificent**, a ship of very similar design and the same class. She was built in the slip beside **Warrior** in Belfast.

Many of the officers in **Warrior** had transferred to "The Maggie", but it was not the same. She was not the ship whose bottom compartments I knew so intimately!

The story is continued from the end of Chapter 4.

But now on a sudden their wild hearts quailed,
A light foot slipped or a swift beat failed;
The dwarf swayed, clutched
—but his hands outflung
At rushing air in their vain clasp clung.
Through the maze of spars, as an evil dream,
He hurtled down with a soaring scream
Through crashing cordage, and battering yard
That still no inch of his fall would guard
To the grunting planks—and they saw on deck
His thighbones crumple about his neck.

The story is continued at the end of Chapter 6.

6. Various Things

Lord, Though hast made this world below the shadow of a dream. An', taught by time, I tak' it so—

"M'Andrew's Hymn" R. **Kipling**

Telford of the Class of 4T3 Engineering

WITH SEA AND SKY AND MACHINERY AS A COMMON BACKDROP, every ship puts its engineer officer to different trials and experiences. Joining **HMCS *Cape Breton*** (part of EG6) for training, Lt(E) Bob Telford RCNVR found himself serving "Curley, a very talented guy, especially when it came to troubleshooting and fixing things". Going on, he says:

"My first assignment was to make a drawing of all the pipes in the ship, sea water, fresh water, steam, air, drains, etc, etc. This was a massive job, and I kept thinking surely there must be plans available somewhere from which the ship was built. The other thought I had was that he was giving me this to keep me busy so I wouldn't get in his hair. Along with this I also did my watch-keeping periods in the boiler room and the engine room; it was very interesting in the way of getting to know a lot of guys from various parts of Canada and from various walks of civilian life.

"The boiler room was both boring and nerve-racking. Most of the time was spent cleaning the

Some of the Probationary Acting Temporary SubLts (E) from the Class of 4T3 Engineering at University of Toronoto, en route to Halifax May 1943. Curzon, Plaxton, Telford, Grosskurth, Aykroyd, Dyke, Moeser, Darling..

burners, but we had quite a bit of trouble with the Weir boiler feed pumps which kept stopping for no apparent reason—and they were a vital piece of equipment. In the engine room, the problem was bearings. I think the ship's triple expansion engines had never been properly lined up when she was built. It wasn't until we had to be laid up in Derry for a longer-than-usual stay that Curley managed to get some old guy from Harland and Wolff to take a look at them. He brought a plumb bob, and scraped and adjusted until he had things running pretty smoothly. It didn't help that after we had spent hours blueing and scraping, the Captain always wanted to make a good impression by steaming out of harbour at 160 rpm. After about an hour of this the bearings were burnt and the engines began to pound and we were dumping oil into the bearings by the bucketful.

"We had some tough trips! On a convoy to Russia, a torpedo went up in our CAT gear, shaking the ship so badly that both turbine-driven generators failed. To get full power back, we had to make some parts on the ship's lathe, at which Curley shone. But the question might have been asked, 'Why didn't we have the parts in stock?'

"After coming back from Russia, because of the torpedo blast, the ship was leaking like a sieve, mainly in the fuel tanks. Repair without dry-docking meant emptying the tanks, and swabbing them dry with cotton rags. An army of little Irishmen went in and worked all day, coming out soaked to the skin with Bunker C oil. What a job, and what a marvellous bunch of workers.

"There were some real characters in the engine room. One always answered the voice pipe from the bridge with 'Miller's Dine and Dance' (his name was Miller!) We had one poor guy who, whenever action stations sounded, would go around to all the others saying 'Are you ready to meet your maker?'

"I soon discovered that everyone wanted to know when we were going back in to harbour. Since this depended on when our next boiler clean was due, or how much fuel we had left, we engineers were always being asked, 'How many hours before our next boiler clean, Chief?', or 'How many days' fuel have we left, Chief?' In those days the intervals between boiler cleanings were spelled out in Admiralty standing orders, and no boiler compounds were prescribed. I think it was the Americans who, by using boiler compounds, were greatly extending the period between cleans, and the Admiralty finally followed suit. By the time I took over *Loch Achanalt* boiler cleans were no longer a factor, and we carried so much fuel that we could stay out for ever.

"Once my watch-keeping days were over, as Engineer Officer in *Loch Achanalt*, life at sea was quite different. We engineers had lots of time on our hands. I played a lot of cribbage with the ship's doctor, and would wander up to the bridge to chat with the other officers there. It was also interesting to read the confidential messages that kept coming in telling about new things the Germans were coming out with, and how we could combat them. Another aspect of being an engineer was that the few days spent in harbour were our busiest time, whereas with the executive officers it was the reverse.

"*Loch Achanalt* was a British frigate on loan to Canada, built in Scotland, and very different from Canadian-built frigates. She was very uncomfortable in rough seas, pounding heavily and shaking the whole ship as the bow came down. We got off to a bad start when the Squid system, which fired six depth bombs over the bow, went off accidentally, and the charges exploded right underneath us. After that, we spent a lot of time in the bilges trying to stop leaks by hammering the plates with hammer and cold chisel. Eventually, though, the leaks got worse in rough seas, and we had to go into dry dock in Holyhead. This turned out to be a difficult period. Having spent all their money, some of the crew resorted to stealing things from local shops, and were arrested. There were other incidents, including the drowning of a dockworker, for which we were blamed, so that by the time we left, both Holyhead and we were glad to see the last of each other! However, we were only about an hour at sea when we were ordered to return immediately to hand over two milk churns which we had taken. Milk churns were the big cans in which milk was delivered to the ship.

"Late in 1944, just weeks after the start of our operational commission, **Loch Achanalt's** sister ship, **HMCS Annan**, got a radar contact which turned out to be a submarine (U1006, H Voigt AGWL). We attacked and sank it. In the engine room, we tried to follow wild commands of Full Ahead, Full Astern, etc. We learned later that at one point it had been decided to ram the submarine, but seeing at the last minute that she was sinking anyway, we went Full Astern and Hard A Port to avoid hitting it and damaging ourselves needlessly. In the engine room we felt the hull of the sinking sub bounce off us. I came up to the quarterdeck a couple of times during the action to see what was going on, but soon went down and was glad of my assigned position because the air was full of 20 mm shells. After it was all over, we picked up some survivors. One of them said that he was confident Germany would win the war, and that he couldn't understand why we were fighting against them instead of joining them against the common enemy, Russia.

"One memory of being an engineer is sort of bittersweet, that of getting up at 5.00 am with an awful headache, getting up steam to leave harbour, and finally going up on the bridge to test the whistle, seeing first a gush of water come out of it and then the desired sound. But then I would survey the dawn with some excitement.

"***Loch Achanalt*** paid off and was mothballed at Southend on the Thames. I was shocked and very worried that my chores included accounting for every loose item on the ship. Many things such as socket wrenches, electric fans, kitchen utensils, and so on had disappeared by walking off the ship. I learned that the phrase 'lost overboard during a storm' could be used extensively. When it came to explaining what had happened to several hundred models of aircraft which had been used to familiarize people with various kinds of aircraft so they could recognize them when they approached, I was baffled. Most of them had, in fact, been given by fellow officers to girl friends brought on board. I went to talk to the EO of the next ship alongside about it and he said, 'Oh! No problem! Just take what you have left, put them in a corrugated paper box and jump on them. Then you can present them as 150 recognition aircraft damaged in rough seas.' When the accountants came aboard with their big ledger books, we offered them drinks and had a good chat before going below to look at my records. They merely turned a few pages, only glancing at them before signing. All my worry had been for naught."

Money

Money was an interesting subject in the Navy as, of course, in all other walks of life. As mentioned above, it struck some of the wardroom officers where it hurt, with the £5 monthly limit on bar expenses. The largest monthly bar bill came in the month of rising from SubLt to Lt, from one stripe on the sleeve to two. This rise was automatic at the end of a year of service, and meant nothing about abilities. But there was a well-established tradition that the wardroom had to be treated when the news of the change came through; the bill that month was all of 6 shillings! We heard that the French Foreign Legion got paid 2d daily, and spent it as follows: 1d on Algerian wine, a ha'penny on women, and the rest frivolously.

Nowadays, £5 would hardly last a day for most people, let alone a month, and other money amounts must be approached with this same appreciation. Two nights spent in the Nova Scotian Hotel on arrival in Halifax cost $6.00 total. Travelling always set one back about $20.00 for reasons that were difficult to figure out. These were serious amounts! One of the reasons for the loss of funds in travelling had to do with baggage, and keeping it along with one's person. Moving from Rosyth to Belfast cost over £1.00 on baggage handling. Actually that move had an interesting incident in the middle of it. Arrived in Glasgow, it was necessary to transfer from Queen Street Station to Buchanan Street, and a porter, a small man wearing a tweed jacket and a tweed cap, offered his services. Up onto one shoulder went the duffle bag, while the other arm held onto a big case; the owner of both items trotted along behind free of burden. Arrived at Buchanan Street, that owner, ignorant of much about these things, made to pay the porter with a half crown. Like all successful entrepreneurs of his type, he immediately made contemptuous reference to the improper and insulting inadequacy of the amount tendered and praiseful reference to the unfaltering help he had been with the immense load. He was right, of course, and got his proper payment.

The Royal Navy

In general all the career people in the Royal Canadian Navy, those who were in the permanent force, spent some time in the Royal Navy's hands. Many of the others did so too. So the question comes up, "Why?", and again, "Was it a Good Thing?" The latter question was asked and answered by the Canadian Government at the end of the 1950s, when most of such ties were discontinued, and there was then no essential tie that bound the RCN to the Royal Navy. The author's views on the questions were developed in a narrow spectrum of people and time, and are expressed only within that perspective. Whether the steps taken at the end of the 1950s were good or bad, timely or stupid, is not at all clear. They were probably both good and timely, but also led to an important serious loss. The loss was that of a deep understanding of what a Navy is and does, an understanding that is not easily developed, and cannot be built on brashness, bravado, and technical ability. The heart must rule.

The Royal Navy was founded by Henry VIII in the 1500s, and it was not long before great traditions began to be built around it. Drake and the Spanish Armada, for example, come to mind immediately. Those traditions were not only of great seamen, great ships and great battles, but also of great injustices. The press-gang and the cat-o'-nine-tails were amongst the terrible things. But somehow, through it all, greatness prevailed, and the Royal Navy became a preeminent force, totally dedicated to its role and function, and enormously able at it. The Royal Navy through some of its history, at least, knew deeply what a Navy is and does.

Trafalgar and all that went with it was the zenith, the apotheosis of that which made the Royal Navy great. When Nelson hoisted his famous signal, "England Expects That Every Man Shall Do His Duty", it was unnecessary. One of the Captains, at the time, in another ship said as much to those on the quarterdeck with him. It was not necessary because Nelson, his Captains, and the whole of the 15,000 men in his fleet knew it at heart with no need to see it at a yardarm, and intended to act on it, and supported Nelson wholeheartedly. The men subscribed totally, whether they were of the pressed half or of the volunteer half. They knew what was at stake, they knew that Nelson's strategy was a winner, and they knew that the Royal Navy would not fail England, knew it in their bones, bred there over generations.

The heroic role in which the Royal Navy was cast, and in which it saw itself, is well-exemplified by the titles of books published about it in the first part of this century: "The Royal Navy: The Sure Shield of Empire", "Rule, Britannia!", "The Flower of England's Garland", "Heart of Oak", "Britain's Glorious Navy", "The Anatomy of British Sea Power". Hmmm. Yes. One of them is different; titled "The Rise and Fall of British Naval Mastery"; it dates the beginning of the fall from absolute greatness at 1897.

The history of the Royal Navy and of Britain was once our history, and we can claim Nelson and Trafalgar as cousins. But did the traditions rub off onto those of us who trained with the Royal Navy? Even deeper, were the traditions still there to be rubbed off? The last title in the previous paragraph suggests that maybe they were not. The answer to the question of the rubbing off of traditions is partially "Yes" and partially "Well-Yes-But". One of the unhappy aspects of traditions is that they tend to become institutionalized and rigid. Unfortunately, some of those unhappy parts were picked up by some of the Canadians in the Royal Navy. Trained in battleships, some of them thought any other kind of warship was rather despicable and below their station in life. It was not a Good Thing for Canada that some of her career naval officers had this opinion and passed on their views to those who had joined for war service only. There was some Nose-In-The-Air behaviour on the part of officers in the permanent force, almost verging on contempt, for those who were in For Hostilities Only. It is probable that these attitudes and behaviours made the Canadian Navy less able than it otherwise could have been, and than it deserved to be, given the great devotion of those who served for hostilities only. But that is not the whole story, for without the small backbone of permanent ratings, petty officers, and officers, trained in the traditions of one of the world's greatest navies, it is doubtful that Canada could have risen to the heights it did as the world's third largest naval force.

It was a small backbone indeed. Before the war, Canada had about 2,000 in total in its professional navy, the Royal Canadian Navy, manning shore establishments and a total of about twelve ships, six of them destroyers. From that nucleus, the RCN grew to 95,000 people and 378 ships in five years; for each of the original people in the permanent force, there came almost fifty others to join them. It is probably true that the professionals were over-disdainful of the volunteers, and the volunteers in turn insufficiently grateful to the professional force. But it is undoubtedly true too that the professionals were overwhelmed by the numbers and by the operational exigencies of the war. The numbers gave them many landsmen to convert into seamen, and the operational exigencies often gave them no time at all to do it with more than the most rudimentary training

The RCN gave one the impression of amateurism in large part, and the RN of a professional force sure of its own eventual success. That really is a lot of poppycock, if viewed closely. At the Battle of Jutland, the professionals of the RN took a terrible defeat, a defeat of their construction, their ammunition, their preparations, their planning, of their admiralty, of their tactics. They retrieved their position only because Germany accepted Jutland as a strategic defeat, and never again ventured forth to risk the loss of their fleet. The Canadian amateurs, by way of contrast, made up almost the whole of the RCN. Together with their few professional shipmates, they did a great job, and carried the brunt of the Battle of the Atlantic. And won it in due course (with much help from the RN, the Air Forces, and the Americans, be it said). The comment on amateurism in the RCN is only to say that the amateurs could have been better supported and strengthened than they were, in general, had there been better leadership at the top with more, much more, of the "Nelson Touch". But that could be totally wrong, coming from only an engineer, buried in the workings of the ships.

One must wonder what the Naval authorities at the Admiralty thought of the Canadian ships serving under their control, especially those of the groups that contained **HMCS** *Qu'Appelle*. Commissioned in February, *Qu'Appelle* had lost two men overboard, and had had some kind of unacceptable crew action by March or April. She was run into by another of her group in August, collided (gently) with a tanker in September, went aground in October, lost a sister ship to stranding in October, had need of several commanding officers in the course of the year. Could the authorities in London have heaved a sigh of relief when she departed for Canadian waters late in the year? Maybe they could, but those who knew the RN intimately have pointed out that it too was responsible for many awful bloomers. Some of those arose from the fact that the training of its officers from a young age was directed at knocking everything out of their heads and replacing it with Navy thoughts. The result was much routine and bureaucratic thinking. This being so, the separation of the RCN in the 1950s was in fact a Good Thing after all!

Nine Hundred and Seventeen Days

Nine Hundred and Seventeen Days. That was the length of the author's stay in the Canadian Naval

Service, according to the official records. The records also classify the time into other various categories, involving seagoing or not, amongst others. The time in **Qu'Appelle** is all classified in the records, effectively, as seagoing. But it really wasn't. The Archives' records contain, for a few months, copies of one Captain's monthly report for **Qu'Appelle**, giving the following information for "Days at Sea" month by month.

			IN HARBOUR –days	
MONTH	AT SEA –days	REPAIRS	OVER 4 hrs. notice	UNDER 4 hrs. notice
May	6	20	5+repairs	
June	22	0	5	3
July	27	0	4	
August	6	19	6+repairs	

The numbers are interesting; over the 120 days of those four months, 61 were spent at sea and 59 in harbour! August is "unfair", inasmuch as the repairs were forced by the collision with **Skeena**. Still. . .

Nine Hundred and Seventeen Days! An immediate question that arises on seeing the number is "What use was it?" And the answer—"For the War Effort it was of virtually no use". In the various places that I found myself, things would have gone along much the same regardless of my presence. In most of them, **Qu'Appelle**, for example, I was along, in large part, to get the Watch-Keeper's Certificate. In **Battler**, I was along for training, in preparation for **HMCS Warrior**.

But, on the other hand, they were positions that had to be filled, and there I was. Fortunately for me.

Should I really say, 'Fortunately for me?' In all Naval services, there are those who serve in glamorous positions, and many more who serve only to support them. In the Boiler Water Treatment sections of various dockyards were devoted men who got no thanks, no accolades from their peers, no mention in the history books. It appears, even, that all record of their activities is gone. Despite their unknown and unrecorded position in the scheme of things, they were important in dealing with the Boiler Cleaning problem, and accounted for a substantial increase of the Hours at Sea for the Canadian Navy, so playing a vital part in the defeat of the U-boat menace. In many other branches and specialties—in ASDIC, radar, research, code-breaking, and so on—there were similarly devoted people, labouring in obscurity. Thank God for them.

My movements were indeed fortunate for me, though, as an individual, for I had not then the maturity to labour in a corner. One of the things that comes very clear in writing a story like this is the gossamer nature of the threads on which the strands of life are woven. In retrospect, in preparing this narrative, many of these gossamer threads become very evident. Had this not happened, or that, or the other, my whole subsequent life would have been different, and the likelihood of each of this, that, or the other happening was tenuous in the extreme. And, of course, had my course been different, that of many other people would also have been different, by association or in consequence. Over a sufficiently long period, in fact, the whole of the world will be different.

I have recently become acquainted with a subject called, intriguingly, 'Chaos Theory'. It is a mathematical discipline that deals with the enormity of eventual effects arising from the smallest of current events. Initially, I wrote "causes", rather than "events", in that sentence. But the events are not causes, except that, in the most general of senses, all things are 'caused' by all prior events. Chaos Theory makes this relationship explicit. Thus, the weather today is the outcome of every last and smallest detail of the state of the world some years ago. In those 917 days of my life in the RCNVR, I began to get a glimpse of a similar truth affecting one's life. The glimpse becomes a full flood of light in retrospect and in writing about the events, for there are endless gossamer threads leading to discharge on a November day in 1945, which lead in turn to all the subsequent events of a fortunate life time. All the latter would have been changed had the November date been different.

As said very early in this narrative, these 917 days were of profound importance in terms of education about people, about how they behave, about what moves them, about how groups work together, about the qualities of leadership, about management, about many of the important things in life. But not about everything. A few years ago, now at a ripe old age by comparison with the war years, I had occasion to need help in getting a tractor out of the woods in the country. My neighbour across the way was a friend.

"Bill," I asked him one day, "will you help me get

my tractor out of the woods to the mechanic?"

"Sure," says Bill. "Just say the word."

Well, I did say the word, but just before we started down the mile and a half track to where the tractor lay, turning to him, I said, "Bill, before we start, we should come to some kind of agreement."

With a puzzled look on his face he asked, "What do you mean?"

"Well," said I, puffed up and businesslike, "we should come to some agreement about how much it will cost."

That produced an immediate and violent explosion. "I'm your neighbour!", he cried, with great emphasis on the word, and repeated his cry twice. About this I did not learn in those two and a half years—or in the long years afterwards, apparently. Bill taught me. It is never too late to learn.

Out of writing this account, another very great fact of life also has become clear. Life is abrupt. In each of the areas of activity that I was involved in during the 917 days, there were other people and there were physical facilities of one kind or another. They can all be characterized as having started and finished abruptly for me and the others involved. While I was there, the society of **Qu'Appelle** contained me and the others who shared it with me. We worked together, lived together, worried together, were a true society. We have all experienced the abruptness of such groups, especially of their termination. We enjoy a holiday in some resort, are part of the society, have lunch one day as was common on the preceding days, but on this day after lunch find ourselves suddenly in a vehicle departing for ever.

It is not only termination that is abrupt, it is all the smaller things that make up the whole of the experience. And once they are over, they are over, they reside in memory only, and that only temporarily. In due course, they are totally expunged from the known experience of the world. But, interestingly, as Chaos Theory so clearly demonstrates, they have their effect in due course, in making the world totally what it would otherwise not have been. But like the Ship's Book in the Archives, like the ship itself, all the little terminations are abrupt, and the final one is both abrupt and complete. Sic transit gloria.

Abbreviations

To simplify the narrative, various abbreviations have been used where they were convenient. They are the following:

His Majesty's Canadian Ship	HMCS
His Majesty's Ship	HMS
Royal Canadian Navy	RCN
Royal Navy	RN
Royal Canadian Naval Volunteer Reserve	RCNVR, or VR
Royal Canadian Naval Reserve	RCNR, or NR
Naval Service Headquarters	NSHQ
Royal Air Force	RAF
Commanding Officer	CO, or Captain
Chief Engineer	Chief
(Chief) Engine Room Artificer	(C)ERA
First Lieutenant	No 1

Lieutenant	Lt
Commander	Cmdr
Stoker	Sto

Stories by Others

The ships of Canada's Navy have been described in a few publications, and there are a number of books which have included references to **Qu'Appelle** and her actions, or to her Captains.

Schull, Joseph, *The Far Distant Ships* (Ottawa: King's Printer, 1950). This is "an official account of the Canadian Naval Operations in the Second World War". As such it covers many things, including the operations of **Qu'Appelle** in the summer months of 1944, giving some detail on Operations Dredger and Kinetic. It has recently been reprinted, but there are errors! The collision of **Skeena** and **Qu'Appelle** during Operation Kinetic, for example, is not reported.

Easton, Alan, *50 North: An Atlantic Battleground* (Toronto; Ryerson, 1963), is surely the best Canadian first-person account from WWII of the life at sea and in action. Easton was Captain in **Saskatchewan**, in the same group as **Qu'Appelle**, and writes about the group experiences on pp232-285. He refers to **Qu'Appelle** and McKillop only as "the Senior Officer", speaking highly of them; the lack of names for various people and some ships is unfortunate. The burdens placed on the commanding officer of a warship are very clear. This book and another, *Escort* by an RN Commanding Officer, Rayner, D.A. (Kimber and Co., 1955), also make manifest the profound qualities of leadership at sea. Easton's book was a bestseller (50,000 copies) through several editions and is now widely available second-hand.

Milner, Marc, *The U-Boat Hunters* (Toronto: U.of T Press, 1994). Pages 145 to 188 give an accurate account of ***Qu'Appelle's*** activities in 1944, adding memorably to the personal account of the same period by Easton. Cmdr Prentice is dealt with well in this book.

Darlington, R and McKee, F, *Canadian Naval Chronicle, 1939-1945* (St Catherine's: Vanwell Publishing, 1998). Darlington and McKee have done a lasting service to Canada with this book, giving in it as complete a story as we are ever likely to have of the exploits of the RCN in WWII. It contains a few errors, which calls for a little caution in using it. (One error, for example, of interest perhaps only to one who served under Cmdr J.D. Birch, is the subversion of Birch's name three times to "Bush" in Chapter 33. Each of ***Qu'Appelle's*** Commanding Officers of 1944 figures one way or another in this book.) Missing is any reference to the collision in Operation Kinetic. Apart from such minor things, it is a great set of stories, and a lasting record of many facts about the providential destruction of U-boats by Canadians.

Ryan, Cornelius, *The Longest Day* (Greenwich, Conn: Fawcett Publications, 1959). This book deals with D-Day, and contains a reference to ***Qu'Appelle*** as having been in the great invasion armada. This was one of the most widely-distributed of books about D-Day.

Smith, Peter, *Hold the Narrow Sea : Naval Warfare in the English Channel 1939-1945* (Annapolis, Md. :

Naval Institute Press, 1984). This book deals briefly with some of the ***Qu'Appelle*** story. He says: "A few stray shots hit ***Qu'Appelle***, without serious damage". This is, maybe, an accurate assessment, in the large picture, though they hardly seemed, in weight and numbers, like 'stray' shots at the time, nor did Easton, seeing them delivered, look on them as such!

Bishop, Arthur, *Courage at Sea* (Toronto: McGraw Hill, 1995). The actions of ***Qu'Appelle*** are covered on several pages, and there is a picture of Prentice at the presentation of the DSO on p.29.

Johnston, Mac, and Black, Dan, *Canada's War at Sea* (Ottawa: Legion Magazine for May/June 1998). Deals again with ***Qu'Appelle***.

Poolman, Kenneth, *Escort Carrier :* **HMS *Vindex*** *at War* (London: Martin Secker and Warburg Ltd, 1983). This book contains several pages about operations in company with ***Qu'Appelle*** in March of 1944, including pictures of ***Qu'Appelle*** from the deck of ***Vindex***.

Lawrence, Hal, "Victory at Sea" (Toronto: McClelland and Stewart, 1989). There is only a passing mention of ***Qu'Appelle***.

Smith, Peter, *Destroyer Leader* (London: New English Library, 1968). This is the story of **HMS *Faulknor*** from end to end. In the course of her career, that of ***Foxhound*** is intimately entangled, the two ships of the Royal Navy's F-Class being very close, and having very similar histories in the same flotilla. ***Foxhound*** became HMCS ***Qu'Appelle*** in February of 1944.

Sarty, Roger, *Canada and the Battle of the Atlantic* (Montreal: Art Global et al, 1998). Here is a book! A combination of coffee-table volume and thorough history, it gives a good understanding of the land-bound politics, financial strictures and struggles of the RCN in the 1930s and the early years of the war. At sea, it recounts many first-hand accounts of events and the weather. In one storm recounted, **HMCS Restigouche** had its mast blown over, and a funnel unseated! That Commander Prentice played no small role in the Atlantic is made very clear. Lt McCully is to be seen (second from right) in the delightful picture of Admiral Nellie's visit to **Restigouche**. The only drawbacks to the book are the absence of names on many of the photographs and of a list of the illustrations, and the unfortunate lack of an index!

Unger, Isaac, *Skeena Aground* (Winnipeg: Isaac Unger, 1992). Isaac Unger's older brother Abe was one of those lost the night **Skeena** grounded. Isaac has compiled a moving and thorough account of the ship and its end.

English, John, *Amazon to Ivanhoe: British Standard Destroyers of the 1930s* (Kendal, England: World Ship Society, 1993). All the River-class ships of the RCN, and their antecedent status in the RN, are well-covered. Unusually, the costs of construction are set out.

Macpherson, Ken, and Burgess, John, *The Ships of Canada's Naval Forces 1910-1981* (Toronto: Collins, 1981). This book gives brief descriptions of all of Canada's vessels, particulars of size, armament, etc, and pictures.

Macpherson, Ken, *The River Class Destroyers of the Royal Canadian Navy* (Toronto: Charles Musson, 1985). This book enlarges on the detail given in the Macpherson/Burgess volume.

Macintyre, Donald, *The Naval War Against Hitler* (New York: Scribner, 1971). Prentice's U–boat kill in *CHAMBLY* is described; it was this action that won him the DSO.

Johnston, Mac, *Corvettes Canada: Convoy Veterans Tell Their True Stories* (Toronto: McGraw Hill, 1994). Several pages are devoted to Cmdr. Prentice, including some source references on p48.

Macbeth, Jack, *Ready, Aye, Ready: An Illustrated History of the Royal Canadian Navy* (Toronto: Key Porter, 1989). There is one page (62) about Prentice's action in *CHAMBLY*, in which he is called "formidable".

Lynch, Thomas G, *Canada's Flowers: History of the Corvettes of Canada* (Halifax: Nimbus Publishing, 1981). This book gives lots of pictures of corvettes at sea and otherwise, and one, surprisingly, of the carrier *HMS Battler*.

Pugsley, William H, *Sailor Remember* (Toronto: Collins, 1948). Pugsley has given hundreds of photographs in this book, the best of its kind on the Canadian Navy. His photographs are dynamic, immediate, accurate, and to be envied. New recruits, on enlisting in the RCNVR, were told that cameras were not allowed, and most of them foolishly heeded the warning. Fortunately for us, Pugsley did not. This book and his other one, *Saints, Devils, and Ordinary Seamen* (Toronto, Collins, 1945), are a great celebration of the spirit of man, the ordinary man of the lower decks.

Bercuson, David, and Herwig, Holger, *Deadly Seas* (Toronto: Random House, 1997). What a book! The story of HMCS *St Croix*, of U305, and of their encounter. *St Croix* was sister ship to *Annapolis*.

Lamb, James, *Corvette Navy* (Toronto, 1977).

Lawrence, Hal, *Tales of the North Atlantic* (Toronto: McClelland and Stewart, 1985). This book tells again some of the story of the Channel and Bay of Biscay operations in which the River Class and Tribal Class destroyers figured.

German, Tony, *The Sea is at Our Gates* (Toronto: McClelland & Stewart Inc., 1990).

Niestlé, Axel, *German U-boat Losses During World War II: Details of Their Destruction* (Annapolis, Md: Naval Institute, 1998). The details include, on both sides, the ships, the commanding officers, the locations, the means, as well as extensive notes.

Wynn, Kenneth, *U-boat Operations of the Second World War: Volumes 1 and 2*, *Case Histories* (Annapolis, Md.: Naval Institute, 1997). A brief, but illuminating, history of every U-boat is given here. It is striking to read the statements of 'Ships Sunk'—large numbers for most of the earlier U-boats, and trailing off to the bald word 'None' for a large fraction of the later ones.

Jenson, Latham B, *Tin Hats, Oilskins & Seaboots* (Toronto: Robin Brass Studio Inc, 2000). Great stories and many illustrations.

Robertson, Heather, *A Terrible Beauty: The Art of Canada at War* (Toronto: James Lorimer & Company, 1977). Aptly titled, this book deals with both World Wars, making very clear the profound pathos and the absolute evil of war. But one of the great paintings is of Potato Peelers at sea (see p 91 here.)

Various: National Archives of Canada. In Record Group 24, the Archives house various naval records from the 39–45 war. The Ship's Book from *Foxhound/*

Qu'Appelle is one of those records. There are many more things. But it is surprising what is not there, too. No records to speak of deal with engineering matters in the Dockyard at Halifax; there is nothing evident on the Boiler Water Treatment business, for example. Nor are any of the engine room logs or Palmer's files from *Qu'Appelle* there. Too bad. The report on the Board of Enquiry into the stranding of **Skeena** is there, though, and was of much use in writing of that event. Many a 'Story by Others' is to be found in the Personnel Records in Ottawa, a repository of records which are open to the public. The author's file extends a little beyond the end of the war, for in 1946 Ottawa's accountants came onto Claire to return around $50.00 of overpayment made to her in December of 1945!

Blair, Clay, *Hitler's U-Boat War* (New York, Modern Library, 1996). This is a very thorough account of all U-boat actions. Of most interest to the *Qu'Appelle* story is the account of sailings into the Channel and Biscay against the Invasion forces.

And finally, two other stories belong here in some way, for they are references to the kind of vessel, and warfare, and people, that caused the Allied Naval effort to take the shape it did, with all its escort vessels, and convoys, and raids of the kind described in the text here. Both are truly remarkable.

One is by W Hirschmann and D Graves *Another Place, Another Time* (Robin Brass Studio, 2004). Hirschmann, at the ripe age of 22, was Chief Engineer of U190! His book describes his life in detail up to the time of his release from custody as a POW, and a few events with Canadian veterans since then. (U190 sank **HMCS** *Esquimalt* in April of 1945.) Great book.

The other is by Lothar-Gunther Buchheim, *U-Boat War* (Bantam Books, 1979). Buchheim was, essentially, a journalist, working in drawings and paintings. "Convinced," he says, "that the reality of the war was not being reflected in the routine dispatches of war correspondents, I was driven to take more than 5000 photos." These two books are full of them and their urgent immediacy. They show the boats, the harbours, the engine rooms, the sea, Dönitz. But most of all they show the boys and the men who bravely, foolishly, devotedly, blindly, competently served the Devil himself and his obscene cause. Totally misguided, most of them died, cheated of life by the Devil. At the time it is likely that few recognized the Devil to be in charge, nor ever raised questions about the nature of the leadership above them, or the rightness of their mission. That is sobering, for how is an ordinary person to recognize the essential quality of the senior leadership? Probably most people who joined the cause in Canada were simply lucky to find themselves, in due course, opposed to the Devil. Most had not recognized it, at least not clearly, on volunteering for service.

Al Purdy's poem "Names"

The views just expressed have been dealt with far far better by that greatest of poets in the English language, Al Purdy. It is titled "Names". While it deals with the subject, it also is much more wide-ranging, and all who are in charge of events, of politics, of institutions

and institutes must take it to heart, and cry. Here it is
in total:

> *Birthing, begetting and dying,*
> *— the great hammers of being,*
> *each one thudding against the skull,*
> *each one obliterating the others —*
>
> *When it was nearly time to die,*
> *Marcus Flavinius, Centurion of*
> *the Second Cohort, Augusta Legion,*
> *by letter to his cousin, Tertullus,*
> *in Rome, concerning rumours of sellouts,*
> *plots, money grubbing, treason there:*
> *"When we left our native soil, Tertullus,*
> *we were told we were going to defend*
> *the sacred rights of the empire and*
> *of the people to whom we bring our*
> *protection and civilization. Please tell*
> *me the rumours I hear of this treachery*
> *at home are not true —" Nevertheless,*
> *observed in the bright glare of history,*
> *the rumours were entirely accurate.*
>
> *When it was nearly time to die,*
> *Oberleutenant Conrad Schmidt, minor*
> *cog in General Erwin Rommel's Afrika*
> *Korps, dying of shrapnel wounds somewhere*
> *between the Quattara Depression and*
> *a little railway station in the Western*
> *Desert called El Alamein — watching blood*
> *drip from his chest in time with the second*

hand of his watch onto dirty gravel,
measuring his remaining life by
its quickly decreasing volume:
remembering
persistent rumours of Jewish death camps,
remembering
a dead friend's opinion that Hitler
was a psychotic monster,
and wondering if he, Conrad Schmidt,
his last years spent in the Panzerarmie,
had wasted his life.

How not to waste your life?
— no reliable information available.
One could mention, in passing:
even the last act of death
provides only a few hints.
Earlier, during that mid-life period
when the senses overwhelm the mind,
and the calendar blossoms days,
and nothing has much urgency,
questions about personal integrity
are often regarded as trivial.
It seems to me these particular names
are synonymous with the question itself,
and remember their names:
Marcus Flavinius, Centurion
of the Augusta Legion;
Conrad Schmidt, Oberleutenant
in the Afrika Korps:
two men about to die,
who spent their last few moments

wondering how they could change things
on the earth they were leaving —

(By permission. Copyright © 1986 Al Purdy)

In the U-boat service of the German Kriegsmarine, there were about 35,000 men. Of that total, almost 30,000 kept Conrad Schmidt company in their death. They went to sea singing, and to bands playing, even to the last days, when they knew they were highly unlikely to return or to survive the voyage. One could suppose in this that they had some of the Kamikaze spirit, and no doubt a similar spirit is to be found in some present-day armed forces. Unfortunately. But some, at least, of those brave men must have thought at the end as Conrad Schmidt did. We in the RCN were lucky to be party to the destruction of the evil they were involved with and so not at all to have wasted our lives.

The story is continued from the end of Chapter 5.

> ... *Solomon saw disaster now*
> *Stand pictured dark on each vacant brow,*
> *The hideous omen dawned and grew*
> *As mad sails bellied and raged and flew.*
> *He leaped from the bridge with a blistering yell;*
> *His arms like flails on their bodies fell,*
> *With kicks and curses and cuffs and blows*
> *A lone typhoon through their midst he goes.*
> *With a capstan bar to the deck he lays*
> *The helmsman now in a proper daze;*
> *Leaps aft, swings on the drunken wheel*
> *Till Kate the touch of his hand can feel.*
> *She pauses; Stock and the men break free,*
> *Swarm to her yards and speedily*
> *While Solomon bellows command and threat*
> *They bind and conquer her. Blind with sweat,*
> *Blown, wrung and weary they stay for ease;*
> *Kate drives once more with the singing breeze.*

Sleavy's story does bring out the crucial impact
of an individual in the midst of crisis. Like Sleavy,
some of the U-boat captains were great leaders,
but the foul and evil nature of their cause
absolutely prohibits according them admiration
and praise of any kind.

7. Guns, Steam, and Leadership

Man was made for joy and woe;
And when this we rightly know
Through the world we safely go.
Joy and woe are woven fine,
A clothing for the soul divine;
"Auguries of Innocence" William Blake

SINCE THE EVENTS TALKED OF IN THIS BOOK the time elapsed is one full quarter of all the years since Trafalgar. All the ships involved in World War II would be as useless and vulnerable in a hostile sea today as **HMS Victory** herself, Nelson's flagship at Trafalgar. I mention Trafalgar because of a history written of the Canadian Navy in the Second World War. The official historian was Joseph Schull, whose account of the Canadian war at sea was published in 1950. He chose to entitle it "The Far Distant Ships", a phrase taken from the characterization of Nelson's blockading ships during the Napoleonic Wars by the historian A.T. Mahan:

"Those far distant, storm-beaten ships, upon which the Grand Army never looked, stood between it and the dominion of the world."

What could more clearly describe Canada's little ships than that title, conferred by the Canadian official historian himself!

Yesterday's ships would certainly seem to be useless as well as vulnerable today. The Guns and Steam of yesterday could accomplish but little today. That they would be highly vulnerable is beyond question. Those ships of yesterday were attacked with guided weapons—glider bombs or acoustic torpedoes. But the guidance systems were primitive indeed, and the record of successes with them was small. Today the Exocet and similar weapons of an even more lethal nature would make short work of destroying the ships of WWII as they then were. But the ships themselves would not necessarily, in consequence, be useless. Leadership must be taken into account, a truth made crystal clear by the action of **HMS *Jervis Bay*** in one of the great events of the war at sea in the darkest days of WWII.

Jervis Bay, an armed merchant cruiser (that is, a merchant ship that had had a few guns installed on deck), was under the command of a Naval Reserve Officer, the kind of officer called by Schull "difficult naval material". She found herself one day between the German pocket battleship ***Admiral Scheer*** and a convoy of merchant vessels. The German ship was at sea as an agent of Nazi evil, a commerce raider, expecting to make short shrift of any convoy that came near its guns, and filling the Admiralty with deep concern. *Jervis Bay*, under her Captain, Fogarty Fegan, Royal Naval Reserve, had no chance at all under the guns of such a ship. But Fegan, in the great tradition from which he came, steered for danger, engaged the battleship, and thwarted its intentions. The contest was, of course, absolutely uneven, and the outcome certain. In the boiler rooms and engine room of **HMS *Jervis Bay***, the stokers and engine room artificers, many of them in the Canadian naval service, heard the rumble of their own inadequate guns, and the terrible noise of incoming fire from **Scheer**, and died. But their objective was achieved, and **Scheer**, thwarted, lost touch with the convoy. For the devotion of his crew both above and below decks, and his own heroism, Fogarty Fegan was awarded, posthumously, the Victoria Cross.

Fogarty Fegan was a leader of men, as were many in Canada's own Far Distant Ships, some of which have been named in this book, whether permanent force, Naval Reserve, or Volunteer Reserve. And, as I have tried to say, the quality of leadership could be found in all levels of rank in those ships. Whether in the ships or serving them ashore, all were engaged in thwarting the Nazi evil.

Author's Notes

1.   Most of the opinions expressed in this book about ships, people, and service were developed and recorded in 1944. Where the opinions given are those of 2006 is, I hope, clear from the context.

2.   Photos when not by author or colleague (by page number and source): 12–National Maritime Museum, number unknown (NU); 19&23–Toronto Evening Telegram 1943 Nov 20; 32–RCN NU; 35–NMM, 32277; 41–NMM, A30025; 42–NMM, A17874; 46–NMM, NU; 51-RCN, A986; 65-*Qu'Appelle* exSto M. Harper; 71-RCN, A991; 79-RCN, A998; 116-exSto M.Harper; 129-RCN, NU; 144-*Skeena* exSto D.German.

3.   Copyright acknowledgment: The author has tried to acknowledge all sources, and will correct any unfortunate omissions in following editions. The header poems are from the following sources: Contents page—from the Stephanie translation used by T. Cahill, "The Gifts of the Jews", (New York: Nan A. Talese/Doubleday, 1998). All others—from the Wavell anthology "Other Men's Flowers" (London: Cape, 1944).

4. Personal acknowledgments: The author has had much conversation and correspondence from one-time shipmates, and others, and is very grateful for it, whether it has turned up in the text or not. In-house help has been very great, what with forbearance, endless proofreading, suggestions, etc. from Claire, and a suggestion for an early total reorganization of Chapter 1 from my daughter-in-law, Marina.

5. *Foxhound/Qu'Appelle* was built alongside *Fortune/Saskatchewan* in John Brown's Clydeside shipyard, the building site of **HMS *Hood*, *Lusitania*, *Queen Mary*, *Queen Elizabeth*, *QE2*, *Britannia*,** and many other vessels which also took part in thwarting the Nazi evil.

Index

Claire at work